Our Family
Book of Days

by Kathleen Finley

A RECORD THROUGH THE YEARS

Foreword by Kathleen O. Chesto

©1997 by Kathleen Finley
All rights reserved. No part of this publication may be reproduced or transmitted in any form or by any means, electronic or mechanical, including photocopy, recording or any information storage and retrieval system, without permission in writing from the publisher.

Living the Good News, Inc.
a division of The Morehouse Group
Editorial Offices
600 Grant Street, Suite 400
Denver, CO 80203

Cover Design and Layout: Val Price
Cover Photograph: Marc Dickey
Cover Photograph Styling: Clive Tyler
Contributing Graphic Artist: Sean Finley

Printed in the United States of America.

All possible care has been taken to ensure the accuracy of the information contained herein. If any errors have accidentally occurred, they will be corrected in subsequent editions, provided notification is sent to the publisher.

ISBN 1-889108-33-2

FOREWORD

Leafing through the tattered, worn pages of my father's Bible searching for well-loved passages for his funeral Mass, we came across three pages originally left blank by the publisher. On the first page, my dad had recorded every family birthday and anniversary; on the other two he had listed each important family event that had occurred since the Bible was purchased. The closing on the home in Florida, visits by his family from Ireland, vacation trips, his new car, even occasional oil changes, all had been carefully preserved in his bold, slanted script. Some of the events were long forgotten, some we had never known, and for some, we had simply failed to understand the significance a father's love could invest. We laughed and cried our way through the treasury of memories he had left us and finished with a profound awareness of the significance of all our lives.

The simple fact that he kept his record in his Bible was my father's bold proclamation that the names and events he had listed were as important as any of those on the printed pages that came before. Sr. Miriam Therese Winter, professor of theology at Hartford Seminary, once suggested to our class that we were living in the times, and telling the stories, of the third testament. The first, the Hebrew or Old Testament, had been about God the Creator, the second, the New Testament, about the Redeemer. The third testament would tell the stories of the Spirit in our world today; the third testament is the testament my father kept on the last three pages of his Bible.

Kathy Finley has encouraged all of us to begin to record and celebrate the sacred events of the third testament. *Our Family Book of Days* offers a guide for becoming aware of all the lives that touch our own, while remembering and celebrating our family's own sacred moments. As the structure for her work, she has wisely chosen the one book every family reads, the calendar.

Each month in this calendar book begins with an introduction filled with suggestions for family rituals to celebrate both important days of the month and moveable feasts and seasons. The suggestions are light-hearted and simple, things an ordinary family might attempt to do, ideas for "real" people that possess the possibility of becoming well-loved family traditions.

Every day of the month lists birthdays, feasts, national holidays, and important events connecting our family to the greater political and religious world. On the birthdays of important political leaders, we can review the legacy they left us. Birthdays of famous authors and musicians offer an invitation to explore their works, and religious feasts suggest celebrating our own heritage or learning a little more about the heritage of others in our multicultural world. These thoroughly researched pages are bound to present some holidays and events that surprise the most knowledgeable among us. The empty space provided each day for the family's own "sacred" moments situates the family firmly within this thoughtfully woven social fabric.

No family will want to celebrate all these events or ideas given, but the multiplicity of suggestions ensures that every family will find the ideas it needs for the rituals that will become a part of their lives. The introduction encourages us to make the choices needed to make the book our own. But even if all we chose to do was to read the entries for each day, we would face each day deeply aware of the events and the lives that have shaped our own. If all we chose to do was to record our own important events, no matter how simple or how foolish they seemed to us at the time, the book would become a priceless treasure in the hands of our children and our children's children.

This is a book that needs to be given to every newly married couple, every new parent, every child leaving home to begin a new life. It is a tribute to the sacredness of all our lives and an invitation to become aware of our days and to celebrate our holiness.

—Kathleen O. Chesto

Introduction

Holy events are happening right before our eyes in our families every day. We may not be used to referring to the constant buzz of family life as holy, but God is there, unmistakably, often disguised in what looks very ordinary until we get out the family album, the box of snapshots, the slide projector or the videos and start to look back. Then what has gone whizzing by begins to take on another perspective and we *remember*. We *recall* together that we are *members* of one another and that God is there in our midst, usually when we least expect it.

This book is designed as a tool to help your family remember and celebrate more easily what is happening in your midst year after year. It is yours in more than the usual sense of the word. Besides the dates already listed here for each day, in order for this to really be your family's *Book of Days*, you will need to fill in the birthdays, weddings, anniversaries, deaths, moves and any other important dates for your family, such as major trips, accidents, illnesses, graduations, etc. You may want to add friends' birthdays and anniversaries as well to serve as reminders to send a card or make a call.

Even seemingly trivial events carry the memories that create your family's special heritage. Did a teenager get a driver's license? Did you have a foreign houseguest? Did someone break a leg? star in a play? cut a tooth? get chickenpox? make a speech? As these events fill your lives, add them here to make this a living record, uniquely yours. Each day, then, has several reasons to celebrate and to remember the years. We have had a homemade version of this book in our kitchen for the last 15 years. It has seen many additions, even the issuing of a new comic book series and the day our cat died.

This book works best if it is checked daily. One way to do that would be to have someone in the family read the entries of the day before a main meal, perhaps dinner. If your family's schedule doesn't allow for everyone gathering daily for a meal, keep it in a place where all can check it daily.

Prayer and ritual in the home shouldn't look "churchy"; our homes are a much less formal environment. But we can become more aware of all the people in our lives and our world that help us to be who we are and help us to see and to know God, who is love, in our midst. *Our Family Book of Days* remembers Christian saints and feast days and includes you in the communion of saints that have gone before. You will also find reminders about U.S. holidays or events; Jewish feasts; important days in countries around the world; birthdays of major writers, musicians, artists, scientists, inventors; and notes about other significant happenings or notable personages that have impacted our world in special ways.

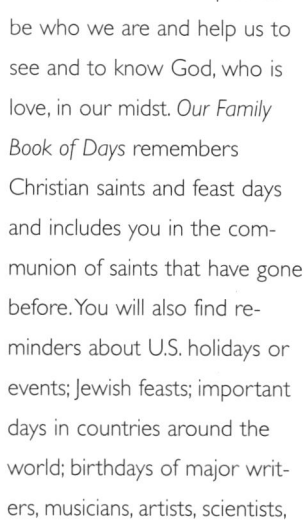

Each month begins with a brief introduction to the highlights of the season and to upcoming floating holidays. This is followed by a section with specific suggestions tied to events within that month. These events are marked with the symbol ❦ reminding you to turn to that month's Celebrating the Day page for an activity idea. These suggestions might be helpful for your family, but there are many other ways to use the information in that particular month. See what works for your family, whose spirituality and needs are unique among other families, just as our individual needs and spiritualities are unique.

Your *Family Book of Days* is designed to help you honor your special interests. For example, we might want to pray for all dentists on the feast day of the patron saint of dentists (St. Apollonia, February 9) or for the people of Sweden or Haiti or Greece or Puerto Rico on an important holiday for them. Celebrate your favorite writers on their birthdays by reading excerpts from their work; go to an art museum and enjoy the paintings of your favorite artists or play some of a composer's or musician's music on their days; tell the stories of global tragedies and triumphs as they are recalled herein.

Perhaps someone in your household would like to make posters or banners for some special days or seasons. Is there an actor or actress in your house who would like to act out a story from scripture or an incident from a famous person's writing? Any time a country or state is mentioned on a day, make it a point to locate it on a map or globe; it will help everyone's sense of geography. Foods are a rich and multisensory way to celebrate, whether a birthday cake or ethnic foods appropriate to the day or season. Experiment as time allows with some unfamiliar foods; you may discover some new family favorites.

Let this book become a part of your lives, not as "one more thing" to have to remember to do, but as a way to deepen your awareness of the days, months and years that slip so easily by. We are rediscovering a deep hunger in all of us for traditions and roots; this book can help the awareness that we're creating memories all the time. All this remembering helps us know that our community—and our God—extends far beyond the walls of our home or our country...we have much to celebrate.

This book owes its existence to many people who helped bring it to birth. Besides the many friends who encouraged me through the years to keep searching for a publisher, Kathy Mulhern has been much more than an editor, offering excitement and encouragement about the need among families for a book like this. The origins of my keeping a homemade book of days in a looseleaf binder go back to Sam Macintosh and a newsletter on family prayer and ritual called "Greenblade" and then later *Family Festivals* magazine in the early 1980's. Sam's vision of family tradition and ritual has been an important inspiration. Canon Kristi Philip of St. John's Episcopal Cathedral in Spokane, Washington was a great help with Episcopal feasts and resources. And last, but certainly not least, my husband, Mitch, and our three sons, Sean, Patrick and Kevin were both supportive and very patient as I finished work on this long-time dream of mine.

LEGEND

✾ A specific suggestion for celebrating this entry can be found in that month's Celebrating the Day page
❖ General information about famous people, places and events
✝ Saint or prominent Christian figure or date (**Note**: Saints and feast days that are only on the Roman calendar are noted as [Catholic]; significant individuals and feast days that are only in the Episcopal calendar are noted as [Episcopal])
✡ Jewish holidays or memorable events
⚖ Event or personage related to the United States
@ Event relating to the global community
♪ Musical composer or performer
⚱ Writer or literary figure
🖼 Artist
⚾ Sports figure or event
💡 Inventor
⚗ Scientist
🚀 Space exploration

JANUARY

January marks our beginnings in the coldest and darkest time of the year and our hopes that spring will return again. Armed with our New Year's resolutions to be kinder, to get in better shape and to take more time to be with one another and with our God, life begins its pace again after the holidays. The new year begins with the Feast of Mary, the Mother of God [Catholic] and the Feast of the Holy Name of Our Lord [Episcopal]. Both feasts invite us to reflect on God's active presence, both in human history and in all our human days.

The Twelve Days of Christmas end on the eve of the traditional date for the Epiphany. Often the Twelfth Night (January 5th) is a time for parties with plays, skits and cakes with prizes baked into them. On Epiphany, the Sunday closest to January 6th, Christians celebrate Jesus' being manifested to the whole world. The wise ones followed the star and gave to the infant gifts of gold, frankincense and myrrh (Matthew 2:1-12), recognizing his kingship. We begin our year acknowledging Jesus as our King, and resolving to seek him out and give him all we are and have. This feast is also called Little Christmas and is a traditional time to bless the house.

Epiphany also reminds us that our God is not just for our families and for those who look and live much like us, but for all the world. Jesus is given as a Light to all the ways that people live, love and suffer. January is a good time to talk together about the differences between us and the unity of love to which we are called in Christ. Who are the "wise ones" from distant lands or foreign ways who can reveal God's glory to you in new ways? Who might live around the corner but be so different from you that you fail to recognize the Light in their lives? Reading *The Best Christmas Pageant Ever* by Barbara Robinson can help start a conversation about such discoveries.

We celebrate the Baptism of the Lord on the first Sunday after Epiphany. Remembering Jesus' baptism helps us to recall our own, with all the promises we have made to God and that God has made to us. This would be a great time to get out family photos of baptisms and talk about how we live out our baptism.

Tu B'shvat, a Jewish holiday that usually falls in late January or early February, is called the New Year's for Trees. The sap begins to rise in the trees and, although winter is not over, life is starting to stir. This holiday is celebrated in Israel by planting trees and in other countries by donating to a fund dedicated to building up Israel's forests. One way to honor this day would be to eat a meal consisting of foods that come from trees, such as fruits and nuts—see how many kinds you can think of. Small children may want to play a game where they imagine that they are a seed growing into a mighty tree or plant. Talk about what kind of tree they want to be, what kind of fruit or nuts they wish to bear, and how it feels to grow so tall and blow in the wind.

Welcome January, with its days of wonder, water and word.

CELEBRATING THE DAY

1 New Year's Day is the time to make resolutions. What is one family resolution you can make and help each other keep through the year? Make it simple, like always putting dirty socks in the laundry basket, or taking good phone messages for each other.

5 When does your family take down the Christmas decorations? Is there a way to choose a date each year and have it be a time of thankfulness for the memories of the season? The eve of Epiphany is one suggestion, since it comes at the end of the traditional twelve days of Christmas.

6 Celebrate the Epiphany, when Jesus was manifested to the whole world through the visit of the wise ones. Have "kings" or "queens" in crowns and robes at your house bring "gifts" while singing "We Three Kings of Orient Are." Try using crowns from a fast food chain with the logo covered over. Or make simple crowns from yellow construction paper, glitter, sequins, markers, etc.

12, 18, 27 This month has several children's authors' birthdays. Why not read "Cinderella," "Sleeping Beauty" or "Little Red Riding Hood" on Charles Perrault's birthday or Pooh stories on A.A. Milne's birthday or part of *Alice's Adventures in Wonderland* on Lewis Carroll's birthday? (Older children might enjoy an Edgar Allen Poe story on his birthday, the **19**th.)

15 Martin Luther King, Jr.'s birthday is a good time to talk about respect for all races and peaceful resolution of conflict, which he taught and lived. Find a copy of his "I Have a Dream" speech at your local library and share some of it with your children. (January **10**th, the anniversaries of the League of Nations and the United Nations, also gives a chance to talk about how world peace can happen.)

21 Don't forget National Hugging Day. Gentle touch is vital to human health. We all need several hugs a day!

25 St. Paul's conversion (related in Acts, chapter 9, as well as in chapters 22 and 26) could be acted out by a family that is dramatically inclined. His blindness and then restored vision after baptism is a strong image of faith.

26 Discover Australia! Find a book or two about Australia and read about this amazing continent. What can you learn about the Aboriginal culture? about its wildlife? about its British connections?

27 Take some time to enjoy the music of Mozart today. "Eine Kleine Nachtmusik" or "The Magic Flute" are good choices, or listen to "The Toy Symphony" by his father Leopold. Older teens could watch the movie *Amadeus*.

29 Are you baseball fans? Guess who might be added to the Hall of Fame this year. On January **31**st we remember Jackie Robinson, the National League's most valuable player in 1949. He had a career batting average of .311 and was elected to the Hall of Fame in 1962. Write to the Baseball Hall of Fame for more baseball facts: P.O. Box 590, Cooperstown, NY 13326.

JANUARY

1

❖ New Year's Day ✿

✝ Feast of Mary, the Mother of God [Catholic] and The Holy Name of Our Lord [Episcopal]

✝ Eighth Day of Christmas

☥ Emancipation Proclamation, 1863, when President Lincoln signed the order declaring no more slavery

☥ Birthdays of Paul Revere (1735–1818) and Betsy Ross (1752–1836), important figures in the American Revolution

@ Independence Day in Haiti, Cameroon, Sudan and Western Samoa

2

✝ Ninth Day of Christmas

✝ Sts. Basil the Great (329–379) and Gregory Nazianzen (329–390), bishops and important teachers in the early Church [Catholic commemoration] See May 9 and June 14

✝ St. Macarius (296–394), patron saint of pastry cooks and confectioners, famous for sugarplums

@ Kakizome festival, Japan, when the first strokes of the year are made on paper with traditional brushes

JANUARY

3

✝ Tenth Day of Christmas
✝ St. Genevieve (422–500?), patron saint of Paris, and of secretaries, actors and lawyers
★ Alaska became the 49th State, 1959
✒ Birthday of J.R.R. Tolkien (1892–1973), author of *The Hobbit* and *The Lord of the Rings* trilogy

4

✝ Eleventh Day of Christmas
✝ St. Elizabeth Seton, mother, wife, teacher, founder of a religious community and first American-born saint (1774–1821) [Catholic]
★ Utah became the 45th State, 1896
✒ Birthday of Jacob Grimm (1785–1863), who with his brother William, published *Grimm's Fairy Tales*
⚗ Birthday of Sir Isaac Newton (1643–1727), physicist and mathematician, discoverer of the law of gravity
❖ Birthday of Louis Braille (1809–1852), educator of the blind who originated the Braille system of printing and writing

JANUARY

5

☦ Twelfth night, end of medieval Christmas festivities and eve of Epiphany ❃

☦ St. John Neumann (1811–1860), Bishop of Philadelphia, known for his extraordinary organizational skills [Catholic]

⚗ Anniversary of the death (1943) of George Washington Carver, black American agricultural scientist, author, inventor and teacher; born into slavery, probably in 1864

6

☦ Traditional date of Epiphany, or "manifestation," when the star led the Magi to the manger at Bethlehem (Matthew 2:1-12) ❃

☦ Blessed Andre Bessette (1845–1937), a humble Brother with a deep devotion to St. Joseph [Catholic]

♜ New Mexico became the 47th State, 1912

✒ Birthday of Carl Sandburg (1878–1967), American poet, historian and biographer of Abraham Lincoln; his *Rootabaga Stories* is a collection of children's stories that have ties to old folk songs

❖ The first around-the-world commercial airlines flight by Pan American Airways, 1942

JANUARY

7

✝ Some Orthodox churches and people in Russia celebrate Christmas on this date
✝ St. Raymond of Penyafort (1175–1275), priest and patron saint of confessors and medical record librarians [Catholic]
☨ Birthday of Millard Fillmore (1800–1874), 13th U.S. President
@ Liberian Pioneers' Day, a holiday in Liberia honoring the 19th-century pioneers who came, mostly from the U.S., to establish a black nation
❖ The first balloon flight across the English Channel, 1785
❖ First commercial bank opened in the U.S. in Philadelphia, 1782

8

@ United Nations' World Literacy Day, to foster universal literacy
@ Midwife's Day or Women's Day in Greece, when the women relax and the men do the housework and look after the children

JANUARY

9

✝ Julia Chester Emery (1852–1922), missionary [Episcopal]

☆ Birthday of Carrie Lane Chapman Catt (1859–1947), founder of the League of Women Voters

☆ Connecticut became the 5th State, 1788

☆ Birthday of Richard Nixon (1913–1994), 37th U.S. President and the only one to resign from office (in 1974)

10

✝ Anniversary of the death of William Laud (1573–1645), Archbishop of Canterbury and Church reformer [Episcopal]

@ League of Nations founded in 1920, after World War I, to avoid war (League dissolved in 1946) ❀

@ First General Assembly of the United Nations held in London, England, 1946, with 51 nations participating ❀

JANUARY

11

☆ Birthday of Alexander Hamilton (1755–1804), American statesman and first Secretary of the Treasury

☙ Birthday of Eugenio Maria de Hostos (1839–1903), Puerto Rican patriot and scholar, commemorated in Puerto Rico

12

✒ Birthday of Jack London (1876–1916), American author of stories of the sea and the far north, including *The Call of the Wild*, which has been translated into 68 languages

✒ Birthday of Charles Perrault (1628–1703), author of stories including "Cinderella," "Sleeping Beauty" and "Little Red Riding Hood" ❀

JANUARY

13

- ✝ St. Hilary (315–368), early bishop and teacher
- ✝ Birthday of Miguel Pro (1891–1927), Mexican Jesuit priest who often used disguises so as not to be caught by the anti-Catholic government but was finally executed by a firing squad [Catholic]
- ☙ St. Knute's Day in Sweden, last day of the Christmas season
- ❖ Traditionally the coldest day of the year

14

- ★ Ratification Day, commemorating the ratification of the Treaty of Paris by the Continental Congress in 1784, establishing the U.S. as a sovereign country
- ✒ Birthday of Albert Schweitzer (1875–1965), author, organist, theologian, medical missionary and recipient of the Nobel Peace Prize in 1956

JANUARY

15

☆ Birthday of Martin Luther King, Jr. (1929–1968), black civil rights leader, minister, author and recipient of the 1964 Nobel Peace Prize (Observed as a legal holiday on the third Monday in January) ✿

@ Adults' Day, or Seijin-No-Hi, in Japan to celebrate those youth who have reached adulthood in the past year

16

☆ Persian Gulf War began, 1991

❖ National Nothing Day, started in 1993 by a newspaperman

17

JANUARY

✝ St. Anthony the Abbot (251–356), hermit and patron saint of butchers, brush makers and domestic animals

✝ Birthday of Thomas Dooley (1927–1961), medical missionary in Southeast Asia [Catholic]

★ Birthday of Benjamin Franklin (1706–1790), printer, statesman, inventor, philosopher and diplomat

★ Denmark sold Danish West Indies (later Virgin Islands) to U.S., 1917

@ Liberation Day in Poland, commemorating the liberation of Warsaw from Nazi oppression in 1945 by Soviet troops

18

✝ Confession of St. Peter the Apostle
   (Matthew 16:13-20)

★ Birthday of Daniel Webster (1782–1852), statesman and orator

♤ Birthday of Alan Alexander (A.A.) Milne (1882–1956), English author best known for his books about Winnie the Pooh
   (also known as Pooh Day) ❀

@ Tunisia National Revolution Day, honoring the movements of the 1930's and 1940's that led to independence in 1956

JANUARY

19

✝ Wulfstan (1008?–1095), monk and bishop
☆ Birthday of Robert E. Lee (1807–1870), Civil War Confederate general
✒ Birthday of Edgar Allen Poe (1809–1849) American poet and short story writer ✽
💡 Birthday of James Watt (1736–1819), Scottish engineer who helped develop the steam engine
   (The watt and kilowatt of power are named for him.)

20

✝ St. Fabian (died 250), pope and martyr
✝ St. Sebastian (257–288?), martyr and patron saint of archers, soldiers, athletes and Rio de Janeiro, Brazil
☆ Presidential Inauguration Day, every four years
@ Babin Den, Grandmother's Day, in Bulgaria
● First basketball game (1892) played in Springfield, Massachusetts

21
JANUARY

✝ St. Agnes (died 258?), virgin and martyr, patron saint of Girl Scouts, all young girls and chastity
♟ Birthday of Thomas Jonathan "Stonewall" Jackson (1824–1863), Civil War Confederate general
❖ National Hugging Day
❖ First Kiwanis Club, a community service organization, began in 1915 in Detroit, Michigan

22

✝ St. Vincent (died 304), deacon and martyr, patron saint of winegrowers
⚗ Birthday of Andre Ampere (1775–1836), physicist, student of electricity and magnets (The ampere, a unit of electric current, is named for him.)
✒ Birthday of George Gordon, Lord Byron (1788–1824), British romantic poet whose masterpiece, the poetic narrative of *Don Juan,* was never finished
✒ Birthday of August Strindberg (1849–1912), Swedish novelist and dramatist
❖ Birthday of Francis Bacon (1561–1626), British statesman and essayist

JANUARY

23

- ✝ Phillips Brooks (1835–1893), American bishop, preacher and author of the hymn "O Little Town of Bethlehem" [Episcopal]
- ★ Birthday of John Hancock (1737–1793), patriot and statesman, first signer of the Declaration of Independence
- @ The Grand Duchess' Birthday, a national holiday in Luxembourg, one of the smallest and oldest independent countries in Europe
- ❖ National Handwriting Day, popularly observed on the birthday of John Hancock to encourage more legible handwriting

24

- ✝ St. Francis de Sales (1567–1622), bishop, teacher and patron saint of authors [Catholic]
- ✒ Birthday of Edith Wharton (1862–1937), American author and Pulitzer prize winner whose book, *The Age of Innocence*, was later made into a movie
- @ Alacitas Fair, La Paz, Bolivia, in honor of the god of prosperity of the Aymara Indians, to whom prayers and offerings are given
- ❖ Gold was discovered at Sutter's Mill in California in 1848; 40,000 prospectors came west

JANUARY

25

✝ Conversion of St. Paul, who was blinded while riding to persecute Christians and heard a voice saying to him, "Saul, Saul, why do you persecute me?" (Acts 9:1-19)

★ First televised Presidential news conference, 1961

✒ Birthday of Robert Burns (1759–1796), beloved Scottish poet and writer of songs such as "Auld Lang Syne"

✒ Birthday of W. Somerset Maugham (1874–1965), English short story writer, novelist and playwright

✒ Birthday of Virginia Woolf (1882–1941), English writer, critic, novelist and women's rights activist

26

✝ Sts. Timothy (died 97?) and Titus (died 94?), early bishops and friends of St. Paul

★ Michigan became the 26th State, 1837

★ Birthday of Douglas MacArthur (1880–1964), World War II general

@ Australia Day, anniversary of the first British settlement in 1788 (observed on the first Monday following this date) ❀

@ Holiday in the Dominican Republic, honoring Juan Pablo Duarte, one of its founders

@ Republic Day, or Basant Panchmi, in India, commemorating the proclamation of the Republic in 1950

JANUARY

27

✝ St. Angela Merici (1470–1540), founder of the Ursuline sisters, a teaching order [Catholic]

✝ St. John Chrysostom (died 407), bishop and preacher [Episcopal commemoration] See September 13

☗ Vietnam War officially ended, 1973

✒ Birthday of Charles Lutwidge Dodgson (Lewis Carroll) (1832–1898), English mathematician and author of *Alice's Adventures in Wonderland* ❀

@ Auschwitz prison camp liberated, 1945

♪ Birthday of Wolfgang Amadeus Mozart (1856–1791), classical composer and musician from the age of three ❀

28

✝ St. Thomas Aquinas (1225–1274), priest and one of the great teachers of the medieval Church

☗ The Space Shuttle *Challenger* exploded just after takeoff, killing all seven crew members aboard, 1986

☗ Coast Guard established, 1915

@ Birthday of Jose Marti (1853–1895), Cuban patriot and writer

❖ National Kazoo Day

JANUARY

29

- Kansas became the 34th State, 1861
- Birthday of Thomas Paine (1737–1809), American Revolutionary propagandist (also called Common Sense Day in honor of one of his writings)
- Birthday of William McKinley (1843–1901), 25th U.S. President
- Birthday of Anton Chekhov (1860–1904), Russian dramatist and short story writer
- Baseball Hall of Fame established, 1936 in Cooperstown, New York (The first five included there were Ty Cobb, Walter Johnson, Christy Mathewson, Honus Wagner and Babe Ruth.)

30

- Feast of the Three Holy Hierarchs: Saint Basil, Saint Gregory and Saint John Chrysostom [Eastern Orthodox]
- Birthday of Franklin Delano Roosevelt (1882–1945), 32nd U.S. President
- Birthday of Barbara Tuchman (1912–1988), Pulitzer prize-winning historian and journalist

31

JANUARY

✝ St. John Bosco (1815–1888), friend of boys, founder of the Salesian order and patron saint of editors [Catholic]
● Birthday of Jackie Robinson (1919–1972), first black to play in major league baseball
♪ Birthday of Franz Schubert (1797–1828), Austrian classical composer
✒ Birthday of Thomas Merton (1915–1968), Trappist monk, poet and author [Catholic]

FEBRUARY

In February we dare to think about spring. The dark, quiet work of winter is almost over; it is time to prepare ourselves for the profusion of colors and scents that come with spring. The word *february* means "purification," and so we begin this month to look forward to Lent and the opportunity to purify ourselves in Easter hope.

Lent usually begins during this month and is preceded in many locales by a time of feasting and carnival. Carnival comes from the Latin *Carne vale*, which literally means "farewell, meat" because in the strict medieval fasts, no meat was eaten during Lent. The day before Ash Wednesday is known as Mardi Gras in French, or Fat Tuesday, in English. This tradition stems from the old custom of using up all traces of fat, dairy products and eggs before Lent, customarily on pancakes or doughnuts eaten on this day.

How can your family encourage each other in their walk with Christ during Lent? Choosing one or two things to work on together can have lasting effects. What simple deeds of kindness can you include in your daily routines with one another? An extra moment to tell about your day? An extra moment to listen? Setting the table without being asked? Cleaning off the dishes? Being home on time? The traditional Lenten disciplines are prayer, fasting and almsgiving. What might these look like in your family?

Fasting can mean choosing one night a week to have a simple meal of soup and bread. Almsgiving can be putting the money you would have spent in your cookie jar and adding to it every dinner the spare change you have in your purses or pockets. At the end of Lent, write a check for the total and send it to your local food bank. Fasting can also apply to other daily habits besides eating. How about fasting from television? or from the newspaper at breakfast?

Add a few minutes of family prayer to your daily or weekly schedule. How about praying together the Our Father after dinner each evening? or reading together a psalm in the mornings? You can remind each other of your Lenten goals by placing a pretzel at everyone's place at the dinner table during this season. The word *pretzel* comes from the Latin *bracellae*, which means "little arms." The pretzel was shaped in the form of arms crossed in prayer, which is an older prayer tradition than folded hands.

The Chinese, or southeast Asian, New Year usually begins this month, celebrated with firecrackers, gifts and much use of red, the color of good fortune. Do you know which animal this year is connected with? Is this the year of the rat, ox, tiger, hare, dragon, snake, horse, sheep, monkey, rooster, dog or pig? You might want to celebrate with some Chinese food and mandarin oranges.

CELEBRATING THE DAY

2 Today we remember the story about Mary and Joseph bringing the infant Jesus to the temple. There they meet two prophets, Simeon and Anna, who recognize Jesus as the light of the world and the hope of all God's people. Many people collect all the candles in their home on this day and pray a simple blessing over them as reminders of the true Light, Jesus. Candles are a helpful way to focus when we pray. If you haven't done so before, consider having a candle in the middle of the table for your meal prayer or at other times when you pray. Turning off other lights helps to focus attention on the candle and on Jesus, who called himself the light of the world and whom we celebrate on this Candlemas Day. One tradition says, "If Candlemas be fair and bright, winter will have another fight, but if Candlemas be dark and rain, winter is gone and will not come again."

3 If anyone has a sore throat, this would be a good day to pray for them and perhaps touch their necks in blessing. It could also be a time to pray that we can speak of one another kindly and use our throats to praise God.

5 In honor of Weatherman's Day and the establishment of the National Weather Service (**9**th), take a couple of minutes each day to give a weather report. Young children may enjoy making a simple weather gauge: make an X on the back of a paper plate; in the four sections, draw a cloud with raindrops, a snowflake, a bright sun, and a tree bent over with wind; cut out an arrow from construction paper and affix it to the center of the paper plate with a paper fastener. Post the gauge on your refrigerator or back door and invite the children to predict the weather each morning.

7 Depending on the ages of your family, you might want to read some of the *Little House on the Prairie* series by Laura Ingalls Wilder today or some of Charles Dickens' writings.

9 In honor of St. Apollonia, say a prayer for your family's dentist. Do you need any new toothbrushes at your house?

11 Thomas Edison helped invent the light bulb. How would our lives be different without electric light and other jobs electricity does for us? How does it feel to be in the dark and how is Jesus the light of the world?

14 Talk about how Jesus is God's valentine to us that says, "I love you this much."

15 This month we remember both Galileo and Copernicus (**19**th), two astronomers who dared to disagree with the whole world. What "facts" do you think might be disproved within your lifetime? What do you strongly believe in though others think you are crazy?

18 On the date a cow was milked in an airplane, each family member should name the silliest thing he or she has ever seen.

23 If Ash Wednesday falls after this date this year, listen to Handel's "Hallelujah Chorus" from *The Messiah* as a majestic way to bid adieu to the word "alleluia." This word is not said in the church during Lent as a reminder of the weeks that focus on Jesus' suffering. Many families write *Alleluia* on a piece of posterboard, decorate it lavishly, wrap it in plastic, and bury it as an Easter "seed."

FEBRUARY

1

- ✝ St. Brigid (died 525), much-beloved saint of Ireland and the British Isles and Abbess of the monastery at Kildare, the first day of Spring in Ireland
- ✒ Birthday of Langston Hughes (1902–1967), black American poet and novelist whose work inspired the Harlem Renaissance
- ★ National Freedom Day, commemorates the signing by President Lincoln of the 13th Amendment abolishing slavery in 1865
- ★ Beginning of Black History Month
- ♪ Birthday of Victor Herbert (1859–1924), American composer of operettas

2

- ✝ Presentation of the Lord or Candlemas Day, when Jesus was brought to the temple 40 days after his birth according to Jewish law (Luke 2:22-24); candles later became part of the feast and are blessed on this day ✤
- ✒ Birthday of James Joyce (1882–1941), Irish poet and novelist
- ★ Treaty of Guadalupe Hidalgo, acquiring Texas, New Mexico, Arizona and California from Mexico, signed 1848
- ❖ Groundhog Day—traditionally, if the groundhog sees his shadow on this day there will be six more weeks of winter

FEBRUARY

3

✝ St. Blase (died 316), bishop and martyr, who is said to have healed a choking boy and is the patron of those with sore throats
✝ St. Anskar (801–865), bishop and missionary to Denmark and Sweden
💡 Anniversary of the death of Johann Gutenberg (1375?–1468), German inventor of moveable type, making modern books possible
♪ "The day the music died"—Buddy Holly, "The Big Bopper" and Richie Valens all killed in a plane crash in 1959
❖ Birthday of Elizabeth Blackwell (1821–1910), first woman doctor in the U.S.

4

✝ Cornelius the Centurion (1st c.), the first Gentile convert to Christianity (Acts 10) and, according to tradition, the first bishop of Caesarea
★ Kosciuszko Day, honors the birth of Tadeusz Kosciuszko, a Polish soldier who fought with the colonists in the American Revolution
★ Birthday of Rosa Parks (1913–), a black woman who, by refusing to give up her bus seat in Montgomery, Alabama in 1955, helped trigger the U.S. civil rights movement
@ Sri Lanka Independence Day, commemorating independence in 1948 from Britain, for the country known until 1972 as Ceylon
❖ Birthday of Charles Lindbergh (1902–1974), American aviator who made the first solo flight across the Atlantic Ocean

FEBRUARY

5

✝ St. Agatha (died 251?), virgin and martyr, patron of Malta, nurses, jewelers and often asked for protection against fire in homes
✝ Martyrs of Japan [Episcopal commemoration] See February 6
@ Mexican Constitution Day, a day to celebrate the adoption of the present constitution, embracing major social reforms, in 1917
● Birthday of Hank Aaron (1934–), baseball great
❖ Weatherman's Day, commemorates the birth of one of America's first weathermen, John Jeffries (1744–1819), a Boston physician who kept detailed records of weather conditions ❀

6

✝ The Martyrs of Japan (St. Paul Miki and Companions) (died 1597), 26 people killed in Nagasaki by the Emperor Tagosama for their faith [Catholic commemoration] See February 5
★ Birthday of Ronald Reagan (1911–), 40th U.S. President
★ Massachusetts became the 6th State, 1788
● Birthday of George Herman (Babe) Ruth (1895–1948), baseball player who held over 50 records at the time of his retirement

7

FEBRUARY

- Birthday of Charles Dickens (1812–1870), English social critic and novelist, best known for *Oliver Twist* and *A Christmas Carol*
- Birthday of Sinclair Lewis (1885–1951), American novelist and social critic
- Birthday of Laura Ingalls Wilder (1867–1957), American author of the *Little House on the Prairie* series

8

- St. Jerome Emiliani (1481–1537), patron of orphans and abandoned children
- Birthday of Jules Verne (1828–1905), French writer of science fiction, including *Twenty Thousand Leagues under the Sea*
- Birthday of William Tecumseh Sherman (1820–1891), Civil War general
- Boy Scouts of America founded, 1910

F E B R U A R Y

9

✝ St. Apollonia (died 249), martyr and patron of dentists and toothaches
★ Birthday of William Henry Harrison (1773–1841), 9th U.S. President
★ Confederate States of America proclaimed, 1861
★ National Weather Service established, 1870

10

✝ St. Scholastica (480–542?), twin sister of
   St. Benedict and founder of the Benedictine nuns
✒ Birthday of Boris Pasternak (1890–1960), Russian poet and novelist whose novel, *Dr. Zhivago*, inspired the movie by the same name

FEBRUARY

11

✝ Our Lady of Lourdes, celebrating Mary's appearances in 1858 to Bernadette Soubirous, a poor French girl, as the Immaculate Conception [Catholic]

💡 Birthday of Thomas Alva Edison (1847–1931), American inventor of many items, including the phonograph and the incandescent lamp ❀

@ Japanese National Foundation Day, commemorating the founding of the nation in 660 B.C. by the first emperor

@ Nelson Mandela released from prison in South Africa after serving over 27 years, 1990

12

🏛 Birthday of Abraham Lincoln (1809–1865), 16th U.S. President

⚗ Birthday of Charles Darwin (1809–1882), English biologist and naturalist

❖ National Association for the Advancement of Colored People (NAACP) established, 1909

FEBRUARY

13

✞ Absalom Jones (1746–1818), black American priest and preacher [Episcopal]

☆ First public school, the Boston Latin School, opened in 1635

☆ First magazine published, *The American Magazine*, 1741

♪ The American Society of Composers, Authors, and Publishers (ASCAP), which helps with music royalties, founded in 1914

14

✞ Sts. Cyril (died 869) and Methodius (died 884), brothers who were teachers and missionaries among the Slavic peoples

✞ Traditional date for St. Valentine (died 270), martyr, though the custom of sending valentines seems to have more to do with this date being a mating day for birds, according to legend, than with the saint ❀

☆ Oregon became the 33rd State, 1859

☆ Arizona became the 48th State, 1912

☆ Birthday of Frederick Douglass (1817–1895), American abolitionist and public speaker, promoted civil rights for freed blacks

❖ Ferris Wheel Day, birthday of George Ferris (1859–1896), who developed the Ferris Wheel for the Chicago World's Fair in 1893

15

F E B R U A R Y

✝ Thomas Bray (died 1730), priest, missionary to America and social reformer [Episcopal]

⚗ Birthday of Galileo Galilei (1564–1642), Italian astronomer, mathematician and physicist ⚛

♀ Birthday of Susan B. Anthony (1820–1906), American abolitionist and pioneer crusader for women's civil rights, temperance and Negro suffrage

♀ The Battleship Maine blown up in Havana harbor in 1898, helping trigger the Spanish-American War

16

@ Lithuanian Independence Day, marking the proclamation of independence for Lithuania in 1918

❖ First daily television news in the U.S. broadcast, 1948

My B-Day Daniel!

FEBRUARY

17

✟ Seven Founders of the Order of Servites (13th century), who withdrew from their comfortable lives in Florence to pray and serve God [Catholic]

❖ Anniversary of the death of Geronimo (1829?–1909), leader of the Chiricahua (Apache) tribe of Native Americans

❖ National Congress of Parents and Teachers founded, 1897

18

@ Gambia Independence Day, commemorating its independence from Britain in 1965

♎ Birthday of Solomon Rabinowitz (pen name: Sholom Aleichem) (1859–1916), Russian author of Yiddish short stories (which became the basis for the play *Fiddler on the Roof*)

🪐 Astronomer Clyde Tombaugh confirmed the existence of the planet Pluto, at Lowell Observatory in Flagstaff, Arizona, 1930

❖ Anniversary of Cow-Milked-While-Flying-in-an-Airplane, remembering the day in 1930 when Elm Farm Ollie became the first cow to fly and be milked in an airplane 🐄

FEBRUARY

19
Birthday of Nicolaus Copernicus (1473–1543), Polish astronomer who first proposed that the earth moved around the sun

20
First American to orbit Earth, John Glenn in 1962

FEBRUARY

21

✝ St. Peter Damian (1007–1072), abbot and bishop in Italy
✝ Birthday of John Henry Newman (1801–1890), English cardinal and author [Catholic]
✒ Birthday of W(ystan) H(ugh) Auden (1907–1973), English-born American poet
🏛 Washington Monument dedicated, 1885
❖ The first U.S. telephone book issued, to residents of New Haven, Connecticut, 1878

22

✝ Chair of Peter, Apostle [Catholic]
🏛 Birthday of George Washington (1732–1799), Commander-in-Chief of the Continental Army and 1st U.S. President (observed on the 3rd Monday in February)
✒ Birthday of Edna St. Vincent Millay (1892–1950), American poet whose collection of poems, *The Harp Weaver and Other Poems*, won the Pulitzer Prize
❖ Birthday of Robert Baden-Powell (1857–1941), founder of the Boy Scouts and Girl Guides

FEBRUARY

23

✝ St. Polycarp (died 156), bishop and martyr
★ Birthday of W.E.B. DuBois (1868–1963), American leader for black equality
♪ Birthday of George Frederic Handel (1685–1759), composer famous for oratorios and operas, including *The Messiah*
@ Guyana Republic Day, commemorating its independence in 1970

24

✝ Saint Matthias the Apostle [Episcopal commemoration]
   See May 14
🖼 Birthday of Winslow Homer (1836–1910), American landscape and seascape painter
@ Estonian National Day, honoring a peace treaty signed in 1920, confirming its independence from Russia

FEBRUARY

25

- Birthday of John Foster Dulles (1888–1959), American statesman
- Birthday of Pierre Renoir (1841–1919), French Impressionist painter

26

- Birthday of Victor Hugo (1802–1885), French author of *Les Misérables* and *The Hunchback of Notre Dame*
- ❖ Birthday of William Frederick "Buffalo Bill" Cody (1846–1917), American plainsman and showman from the Old West
- ❖ Grand Canyon established as a National Park, 1919
- ❖ World Trade Center in New York City bombed, 1993

FEBRUARY

27

✝ George Herbert (1593–1633), Anglican priest and poet [Episcopal]

⚔ Persian Gulf War ends, 1991

✒ Birthday of Henry Wadsworth Longfellow (1807–1882), American poet whose narrative poems include *Evangeline*, *Hiawatha* and *The Courtship of Miles Standish*

@ Independence Day, Dominican Republic, celebrating Haiti's withdrawal in 1844

✒ Birthday of John Steinbeck (1902–1968), American novelist, whose most well-known works include *East of Eden* and *Grapes of Wrath*, recipient of the Nobel Prize in Literature (1962)

28

✒ Birthday of Michel de Montaigne (1533–1592), French writer and the first to use the term "essay"

❖ Floral Design Day, a day to commemorate floral design as an art form

❖ Birthday of Mary Lyon (1797–1849), a pioneer in higher education for women

29

FEBRUARY

♪ Birthday of Gioacchino Antonio Rossini (1792–1868), Italian operatic composer
❖ Leap Year Day, which occurs every four years to bring our (Gregorian) calendar into closer accord with the earth's actual orbit
❖ Bachelor's Day, on which unmarried men are no longer fair game for dates or marriage

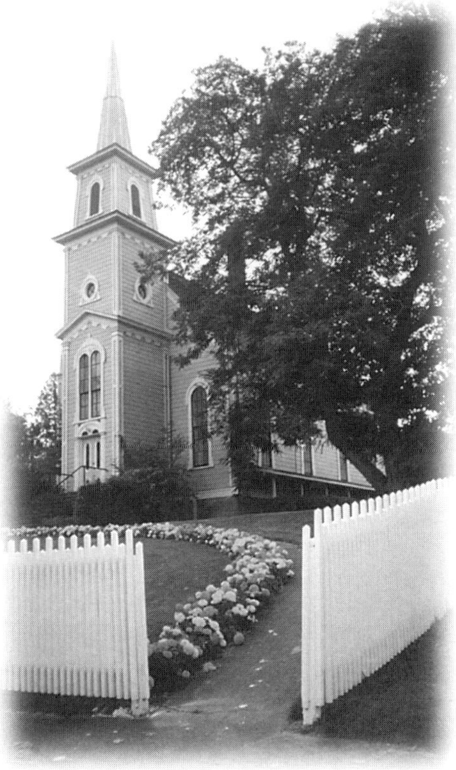

MARCH

March is a blustery time when spring begins and green seems to pop up everywhere. Usually most of the month is taken up with the season of Lent, whose name comes from the *lengthening* of each passing day. The vernal, or spring, equinox occurs around the 21st of the month when light and dark are in equal balance. As we pass the equinox, the days start becoming longer than the nights. (Occasionally Easter falls in March; for Easter themes and ideas, read the introduction to the month of April.)

The six weeks of Lent can be a long time for us to remember to prepare for Easter, so it's helpful to plan for ways to mark each day or week. One good way would be to take a walk every Sunday and look for signs of the "dead" earth coming back to life. (Little people are especially good at this since they are closer to the ground.)

Putting a sign of "death into life" in a prominent place in your home also helps. Try planting some flower seeds in a small pot and setting it on your kitchen table. Make the act of watering it an act of prayer by having the person who waters it say, "Come Lord Jesus, and bring us new life," or some other simple prayer. Or put a dead branch in a pot of sand and add simple tissue paper flowers to it throughout Lent. Children can add a flower each time they remember an act of kindness toward each other.

The Jewish feast of Purim always falls one month before Passover. This is one of the happiest Jewish celebrations since it celebrates the triumph of the beautiful queen Esther over the wicked Haman. This would be a great time to read the book of Esther as a family...or even act it out. Haman, riddled with hatred for Mordecai, an official at the Persian court and Esther's uncle, plotted to kill all the Jews living in Persia. He threw lots (dice known as *purim*) to determine the date for the massacre. Many Jewish communities read the story dramatically, booing each time Haman is mentioned and cheering for Mordecai and Queen Esther.

Though Purim is a day of joy, more recently it has also become a day of somber reflection on the realities of antisemitism. Many Jewish communities take time on the Sabbath before Purim to recall all the other "Hamans" in history who have desired the death of the Jewish people. Purim is a day to remember Queen Esther's courage and pray for God's deliverance for Jews today. Consider taking time to introduce the subject of antisemitism to older children. Encourage them to share stories of any prejudice or racism that they have witnessed. Talk about what you can do to protect human rights for all people.

As the month of March nears its end, Christians mark the Feast of the Annunciation (the 25th), the day we remember the angel Gabriel's visit to the Virgin Mary. In Sweden, the swans are said to return from their winter grounds in the south on this date. Children in Sweden hang up stockings on the 24th and in the morning find candy—"swan's eggs"—which the swans have brought with them to celebrate.

The fifth Sunday of Lent is also called Carlings Day. "Carlings" is an old name for green peas, one of the earliest crops to be harvested in the spring. You may want to have peas for dinner on this night to celebrate spring's approach.

CELEBRATING THE DAY

1 Because St. David is said to have lived on leeks, some families have leek soup for dinner or display daffodils, a relative of the leek.

2, 8, 31 How about reading some of Dr. Seuss's books, which are always a favorite, on the **2**nd or *The Wind in the Willows* on the **8**th for Kenneth Grahame's birthday? Don't forget the excellent collections of fairy tales from various countries—usually titles with colors like *The Blue Fairy Tale Book*—by Andrew Lang for the **31**st!

3, 10 This month we celebrate Alexander Graham Bell and the invention of the telephone. Call someone that you haven't talked to in a while and tell them how special they are.

7 On the birthday of Luther Burbank, you might want to start thinking about and ordering some seeds for your garden this summer.

9 To celebrate Skylark Day, one Russian tradition is to bake rolls in the form of birds to celebrate the return of the skylarks and spring. Shape refrigerated croissant roll dough into simple birds and bake.

10 On the anniversary of Harriet Tubman's death, talk about the Underground Railroad. What was it and why was it necessary? Read more in *Harriet and the Promised Land*, by Jacob Lawrence, or *Follow the Drinking Gourd*, by Jeanette Winter.

13 On the anniversary of the discovery of the planet Uranus, can you name all the planets in our solar system…in order?

17 How many pieces of green clothing can you wear today? Pray for the people of Ireland and for peace in their land.

18 How many diesel trucks and cars can you spot today?

19 Read about St. Joseph in Matthew 1:18-25. What kind of man was he? Why do you think God picked him to be Jesus' foster father?

22 Visit your library and ask the librarian to help you pick out one or two Caldecott winners to read on this day. Imagine an award given every year in your name. Who would you give it to?

21, 23, 31 Play some music of J.S. Bach on the **21**st or some Haydn on the **31**st. Listen to some of Handel's *Messiah* on the **23**rd.

24 With junior high or older children rent and watch the video *Romero*.

26 This is your big chance…a holiday to celebrate that special occasion that just doesn't seem to fit on other holidays! What is it? How will you celebrate? What will you call it?

30 Pray for doctors today and all they do to help us stay healthy and well.

MARCH

1

- ☦ St. David (520–589), abbot and bishop, patron of Wales and poets
- ★ Ohio became the 17th State, 1803
- ★ Nebraska became the 37th State, 1867
- ★ Peace Corps established, 1961
- ★ Yellowstone established as the first National Park, 1872
- ♪ Birthday of Frederic Chopin (1810–1849), Polish pianist and composer

2

- ☦ Chad (died 672), early bishop in Britain, renowned for his deep humility and knowledge of scripture
- ★ Birthday of Sam Houston (1793–1863), American frontier hero and statesman after whom Houston, Texas was named
- ★ Texas Independence Day, declared independent of Mexico in 1836
- @ Independence Day in Morocco, commemorating sovereignty established, 1956
- ✒ Birthday of Theodore Geisel (Dr. Seuss) (1904–1991), American children's author of *The Cat in the Hat* and *How The Grinch Stole Christmas*

MARCH

3

✝ St. Katherine Drexel (1858–1955), an heiress who founded an order of sisters who work with native and black Americans [Catholic]

✝ John and Charles Wesley [Episcopal] See June 17 (John) and December 18 (Charles)

💡 Birthday of Alexander Graham Bell (1847–1922), Scotch-born American scientist, inventor and teacher of the deaf

★ Florida became the 27th State, 1845

@ Dolls' Festival, Hina Matsuri, in Japan honoring little girls and their dolls

@ Morocco Festival of the Throne, to mark King Hassan II's assuming the throne, 1961

@ Malawi Martyrs' Day, honoring the nation's heroes

4

✝ St. Casimir (1458–1483), patron saint of Poland and Lithuania

★ Vermont became the 14th State, 1791

★ Constitution Day, which went into effect on this day in 1789

♪ Birthday of Antonio Vivaldi (1678–1741), Italian composer of *The Four Seasons* and many other pieces

● Birthday of Knute Rockne (1888–1931), famed American football coach

MARCH

5

- ☥ The Boston Massacre, an attack on American colonists by British troops, 1770
- ☥ Crispus Attucks, black American Revolutionary leader, died in 1770
- ❖ Mother-in-Law Day, first celebrated in 1934

6

- ✝ The Missionary Society of St. Paul, or the Paulists, established, 1858 [Catholic]
- ⚱ Birthday of Elizabeth Barrett Browning (1806–1861), English poet whose greatest work, *Sonnets from the Portuguese*, speaks of her love for her husband and fellow-poet, Robert Browning
- 🖼 Birthday of Michelangelo Buonarroti (1475–1564), Italian sculptor, painter, architect and poet, one of the greatest artists the world has ever known
- ☺ Ghana Independence Day, when the then Gold Coast was declared sovereign, 1957
- ☺ Guam discovered on this day in 1521
- ❖ Alamo Day, the end of the siege of the Alamo by Mexicans, 1836

MARCH

7

- ☦ Sts. Perpetua and Felicity (died 203?), a noblewoman and a slavewoman, both young mothers and martyrs for their faith
- Birthday of Luther Burbank (1849–1926), American horticulturalist and plant breeder
- Birthday of Tomas G. Masaryk (1850–1937), Czech patriot called the Father of Czechoslovakia

8

- ☦ St. John of God (1495–1550), patron saint of hospitals and booksellers and founder of the Brothers Hospitallers, a religious order [Catholic]
- Birthday of Kenneth Grahame (1859–1932), English banker and author of *The Wind in the Willows*
- Birthday of Oliver Wendell Holmes, Jr. (1841–1935), American jurist and Supreme Court justice
- Syrian Independence Day, commemorating independence in 1963
- Birthday of Joseph Lee (1862–1937), American developer of playgrounds
- International Women's Day in many countries

M A R C H

9

† St. Frances of Rome (1384–1440), model for housewives and widows and patron of motorists

† St. Gregory of Nyssa (334?–394?), bishop, theologian and brother of St Basil the Great

@ Skylark day in Russia

❖ Birthday of Amerigo Vespucci (1454–1512), Italian navigator and explorer, for whom the Americas are named

10

☥ Anniversary of the death of Harriet Tubman (1820–1913), American abolitionist, escaped slave and organizer of the Underground Railroad

💡 Alexander Graham Bell invented the telephone, in 1876, by transmitting the message, "Mr. Watson, come here. I want you"

❖ Anniversary of the arrival of the Salvation Army in the U.S., 1880

MARCH

11

❖ The Women's Medical College of Pennsylvania, the first medical school for women in the world, incorporated 1850

12

✝ St. Gregory the Great (540–604), Bishop of Rome
   [Episcopal commemoration] See September 3
@ Moshoeshoe's Day, honoring the 19th-century tribal leader of the Basotho people, who now comprise the country of Lesotho
@ Birthday of Kemal Ataturk (1880–1938), Turkish leader and 1st president
@ Mauritius Independence Day, commemorating independence in 1968
❖ Girl Scouts Day, the anniversary of its founding, 1912

13

MARCH

- Birthday of Joseph Priestley (1733–1804), English discoverer of oxygen
- The planet Uranus discovered by German-English astronomer, Sir William Herschel, 1781
- Anniversary of the dedication of Christ of the Andes, a bronze statue of Christ on the Argentina-Chile border, 1904
- The Gutenberg Bible first printed, 1462

14

- Birthday of Albert Einstein (1879–1955), German-Swiss-American father of contemporary physics
- American Eli Whitney was granted a patent for the cotton gin, 1794
- Birthday of Casey Jones (1864–1900), American railroad engineer
- Birthday of Lucy Hobbs Taylor (1833–1910), first woman in America to receive a degree in dentistry

15

MARCH

✝ St. Louise de Marillac (1591–1660), co-founder of the Sisters of Charity [Catholic]

★ Birthday of Andrew Jackson (1767–1845), 7th U.S. President

★ Maine became the 23rd State, 1820

❖ Buzzard Day, the traditional day for the return of the buzzards to Hinckley, Ohio for the mating season

❖ Anniversary of the riots in the Watts area of Los Angeles in 1966

❖ Ides of March, commemorating the assassination of Julius Caesar, 44 B.C.

16

★ Birthday of James Madison (1751–1836),
  4th U.S. President

⚗ The first flight of a liquid-fueled rocket, developed by Robert Goddard, 1926

🚀 The first docking of one space ship with another, by U.S. astronauts, 1966

❖ My Lai Massacre in Vietnam, 1968

❖ The first black newspaper, *Freedom's Journal*, founded in the U.S. in New York City, 1827

17

MARCH

✝ St. Patrick (389?–461?), bishop and patron saint of Ireland

✝ Joseph of Arimathea [Catholic commemoration], a disciple of Jesus in whose tomb he was buried (Matthew 27:57–60) See July 31

🖼 Birthday of Kate Greenaway (1846–1901), English watercolor artist whose drawings of children served as a model for book illustrations

❖ Camp Fire Girls Founders Day, commemorating the founding in 1910

🖼 Anniversary of the opening of the National Gallery of Art in Washington, D.C., 1941

18

✝ St. Cyril of Jerusalem (315?–386), early bishop and teacher

🎖 Birthday of Grover Cleveland (1837–1908), 22nd and 24th U.S. President

💡 Birthday of Rudolph Diesel (1858–1913), German engineer and developer of the diesel engine

🎵 Birthday of Nikolai Rimski-Korsakov (1844–1908), Russian composer

🪐 First space walk by Soviet cosmonaut Alexei Leonov, 1965

❖ The first electric razor was marketed, 1931

19

MARCH

✝ St. Joseph, husband of Mary and patron of carpenters and cabinetmakers, of a happy death and of the universal Church

⚖ Birthday of William Jennings Bryan (1860–1925), American lawyer and political leader

❖ Swallows Day on which the swallows traditionally return to the San Juan Capistrano Mission in California

❖ Birthday of Wyatt Earp (1848–1929), legendary figure of the Old West

20

✝ St. Cuthbert (625–687), English monk and bishop

@ Independence Day in Tunisia, anniversary of a treaty with France, 1956

📖 Birthday of Mitsumasa Anno (1926–), Japanese illustrator of children's books, including *Anno's Journey* and *Anno's Alphabet*

❖ Birthday of Fred (Mr.) Rogers (1928–), children's television personality and advocate

21

MARCH

✝ Thomas Ken (1637–1711), Anglican bishop and hymn writer whose doxology, "Praise God from whom all blessings flow," is sung regularly in many churches [Episcopal]

♪ Birthday of Johann Sebastian Bach (1685–1750), German composer and instrumentalist, one of the foremost musicians of all time ❀

@ Birthday of Benito Juarez (1806–1872), Mexican lawyer, 1st President of Mexico of Indian descent and national hero

💡 Arthur L. Schalow and Charles H. Townes granted patent for the laser, 1958

❖ International Children's Poetry Day

22

✝ James de Koven (1831–1879), American priest and reformer [Episcopal]

🖼 Birthday of Randolph Caldecott (1846–1886), English artist and illustrator for whom the Caldecott Medal is named, given every year to the best picture book for American children ❀

🖼 Birthday of Sir Anthony Van Dyck (1599–1641), Flemish portrait painter

@ Arab League Day, formed in 1945 (The league includes Egypt, Iraq, Saudi Arabia, Lebanon, Syria and Yemen)

@ Slavery abolished in Puerto Rico, 1873

23

M A R C H

✞ St. Turibius of Mogrovejo (1538–1606), bishop in Peru and one of the first known saints of the New World [Catholic]

✞ St. Gregory the Illuminator (257–332?), bishop and missionary to Armenia

♪ First performance of Handel's *Messiah*, 1743 ❀

@ Pakistan Day, when Pakistan was first established as a country, 1956

@ World Meteorological Organization established, 1950, to coordinate weather observations and data

24

✞ Archbishop Oscar Romero of El Salvador (1917–1980), killed for speaking out on behalf of the poor in his country [Catholic] ❀

☦ Agriculture Day, a day of recognition of U.S. farmers, ranchers and growers

@ Philippine Independence Day, achieved in 1946

❖ The oil tanker *Exxon Valdez* ran aground off the coast of Alaska, spilling 11 million gallons of oil into the natural habitat, 1989

25

M A R C H

✝ Annunciation of the Lord, celebrating Gabriel's announcement to Mary that she would be the mother of Jesus (Luke 1:26–38) (Until the calendar changed in 1752 this was the New Year and was celebrated for eight days—until April 1—with gifts and greetings. When things changed, those who followed the old customs seemed foolish, "April Fools.")

@ Greek Independence Day, to honor Greece's independence since 1821

♪ Birthday of Bela Bartok (1881–1945), Hungarian composer

✒ Birthday of Flannery O'Connor (1925–1964), American Catholic writer, author of *Wise Blood* and *The Violent Bear It Away*

26

✒ Birthday of Robert Frost (1874–1963), American poet whose work includes the popular poems, "The Road Not Taken" and "Stopping by Woods on a Snowy Evening"

@ Independence Day in Bangladesh, first declared in 1971

✒ Birthday of Tennessee Williams (1911–1983), American playwright, author of *The Glass Menagerie* and *A Streetcar Named Desire*, which won the Pulitzer Prize

❖ Make Up Your Own Holiday Day, a day you may name for whatever you wish ❀

MARCH

27

✝ Charles Henry Brent (1862–1929), missionary bishop of the Philippines and worker for Christian unity [Episcopal]
⚗ Birthday of Wilhelm Roentgen (1845–1923), German scientist who discovered the x-ray and received the Nobel Prize in physics
❖ Major earthquake in Alaska, 1964

28

@ Teachers' Day in Czechoslovakia, commemorating the life and work of John Comenius, 17th-century Moravian educational reformer
❖ Nuclear power accident at Three Mile Island in Pennsylvania, 1979

29

MARCH

✝ John Keble (1792–1866), Anglican priest and leader of the Oxford Movement, which emphasized the ancient sacramental life of the Church [Episcopal]

☆ Birthday of John Tyler (1790–1862), 10th U.S. President

☆ Vietnam Veterans' Day, when American forces withdrew from Vietnam, 1973

@ Taiwan Martyrs' Day and Youth Day, a day of tribute to martyrs and young adults in the Republic of China

❖ Knights of Columbus chartered, 1882

30

🖼 Birthday of Vincent Van Gogh (1853–1890), Dutch post-impressionist painter

🖼 Birthday of Francisco Jose de Goya (1746–1828), Spanish painter

☆ Alaska purchased from Russia, 1867

❖ Anesthetic (ether) first used in surgery by Dr. Crawford W. Long, 1842

❖ Doctors' Day because of the above ❀

31

MARCH

† John Donne (1572?–1631), Anglican priest and poet who wrote "Death Be Not Proud" [Episcopal]

💡 Birthday of Robert von Bunsen (1811–1899), inventor of the Bunsen burner for chemistry

♪ Birthday of Franz Joseph Haydn (1732–1809), Austrian composer ✿

⚱ Birthday of Andrew Lang (1844–1912), Scottish author famous for collections of fairy tales and folklore ✿

❖ Birthday of Robert Ross McBurney (1837–1898), American YMCA leader

❖ Birthday of Cesar Chavez (1927–1994), American farm labor organizer

❖ Birthday of Rene Descartes (1596–1650), French mathematician and philosopher, called the Father of Modern Philosophy and remembered for his axiom "I think, therefore I am"

APRIL

April brings us Easter and Passover and myriad chances to rejoice in all the new life around us. All of creation sings of God's faithfulness and tender care.

Palm Sunday marks the beginning of Holy Week. The story of Jesus' procession into Jerusalem (Matthew 21:1-9) is a good reason for a parade, complete with palms (if you have them) and any rhythm instruments, including pots and pans. Any music with a good march beat that includes the word *Hosanna* in it would be good, or try "When the Saints Go Marching In." In Eastern Christian churches, the day before Palm Sunday is know as Lazarus Saturday, and the story of raising Lazarus from the dead is read (John 11:1-44).

The Easter Triduum, the three holiest days in the Christian calendar, is Holy Thursday, Good Friday and Holy Saturday. Holy Thursday, also called Maundy Thursday after the Latin word *mandatum* meaning commandment, is the night we remember Jesus' Last Supper with his disciples when he washed their feet and gave them the new commandment (Luke 22:7-34; John 13:1-17, 31-35).

On Good Friday we remember Jesus' death on the cross (John 19:1-37). This is a day of mourning and fasting, a day when we spend time thinking about Jesus' suffering and the love that was poured out for us on Calvary. Holy Saturday is usually a day of quiet preparation for Jesus' resurrection and a day to welcome new members in the community through baptism. The Easter Vigil begins in the evening on this day, and we gather to hear the great stories of scripture through which we recall all God's great saving work for us through history.

These days can be celebrated at home as well as with a community. Share some flatbread or matzah on Thursday and talk about what it would have been like to have Jesus kneel before you and wash your feet. Read the passion account and act it out on Friday. Keep silence in your home: no television or radio on that day.

Saturday is a good day to remember your own baptism. Pull out family photos; read the vows that were made; talk about the baptismal symbolism of dying and rising with Christ. If you buried the Alleluia (see February), Sunday morning is the time to dig it up and proclaim that New Life has triumphed over Death.

Holy Week is full of the themes of the Jewish Passover, a feast that usually occurs this month. This celebration recalls the exodus of the Jewish people from oppression in Egypt. The Seder meal, on the eve of Passover, is a time to remember through story, special foods and decorations, songs and prayers why "this night is different from all other nights." On Passover night, the angel of death passed over God's people. You can read the story in Exodus 12.

Arbor Day is the last Friday in most states and many foreign countries. It is a time to pay special attention to the trees of the world and to appreciate all they add to our lives. An appropriate prayer is from Psalm 96: "O sing to the LORD a new song; sing to the LORD, all the earth. Let the heavens be glad, and let the earth rejoice; let the sea roar, and all that fills it; let the field exult, and everything in it. Then shall all the trees of the forest sing for joy before the LORD; for he is coming, for he is coming to judge the earth."

CELEBRATING THE DAY

2, 3 On the anniversary of the establishment of the U.S. Mint, talk about money and how it's made. How many kinds of currency from other countries can you name? If you have any foreign money, take a look at it. You may also want to read some stories by Hans Christian Andersen and Washington Irving, both great storytellers, on these days.

6 Hold your own family Olympics. Set up some simple events, like running around your backyard or seeing who can jump the farthest or having a jump rope contest. Children would enjoy making the medals. Make sure everyone wins!

8 On the birthday of Buddha older children might enjoy the video *Little Buddha* to better understand Buddhism.

9 In honor of the first public library opening, why not visit yours and "check out" what's there?

12 Celebrate Beverly Cleary's birthday by reading some of her many books about Ramona or Henry or Ralph the Mouse.

14 Learn more about Anne Sullivan and Helen Keller. Rent *The Miracle Worker* or check out Keller's autobiography *The Story of My Life*.

16 Celebrate the courage and creativity of the Wright brothers by making a fleet of paper airplanes and seeing whose stays in the air the longest. Then talk about some of the "silly" or "impossible" things people try to do today, and whether they'll become a reality some day.

21 What is/was kindergarten like for each of the members of your family? Tell what you remember.

21, 22 Earth Day and the birthday of John Muir remind us how precious our environment is to us and how we must work to preserve it. What have you done or can you do at your house and in your neighborhood to help preserve the environment, from recycling to composting? What do we all need to do to keep our air and water and land from being polluted? Talk about your ideas and your concerns about the earth.

26 John James Audubon observed a great deal about birds and then painted them beautifully. The society named after him likes to watch and identify birds. How many kinds of birds can you identify that live near you?

APRIL

1

- Frederick Denison Maurice (1805–1872), Anglican priest and social reformer [Episcopal]
- Birthday of William Harvey (1578–1657), English physician, anatomist and physiologist, who discovered the circulation of the blood
- Birthday of Sergei Rachmaninoff (1873–1943), Russian pianist and composer
- April Fools Day, a day of practical jokes and humor, also called Huntigowok Day (Scotland), April Noddy (England), and Fooling the April Fish Day (France)—See March 25

2

- St. Francis of Paola (1416–1507), hermit and patron saint of sailors
- James Lloyd Breck (1818–1876), American priest and missionary, founder of Nashotah House and Seabury Divinity School, known as the "Apostle of the Wilderness" [Episcopal]
- United States Mint established, 1792
- Birthday of Frederic Auguste Bartholdi (1834–1904), French sculptor of the Statue of Liberty
- Birthday of Hans Christian Andersen (1805–1875), Danish writer best known for fairy and folk tales, including "The Ugly Duckling" and "The Emperor's New Clothes"
- International Children's Book Day, because of the above birthday

APRIL

3

☥ St. Richard of Chichester (1197?–1253), English bishop whose well-loved prayer is remembered:
"Dear Lord, of thee three things I pray: To see thee more clearly, Love thee more dearly, Follow thee more nearly." [Episcopal]

⚱ Birthday of Washington Irving (1783–1859), American storyteller, best known for the legends of Rip Van Winkle and Ichabod Crane ❀

❖ Anniversary of the beginning of the Pony Express, 1860

4

☥ St. Isidore of Seville (560?–636), bishop and teacher who filled his house with the poor

☥ St. Benedict the Moor (1526–1589), patron saint of black North Americans whose love of service was best expressed through the kitchen [Catholic]

☩ Martin Luther King, Jr., assassinated, 1968

@ Liberation Day in Hungary, celebrating the end of German occupation, 1945

@ Senegalese National Day, celebrating sovereignty in 1960

⚱ Birthday of Maya Angelou (1928–), American writer and poet

❖ Birthday of Dorothea Dix (1802–1887), American social reformer

❖ North American Treaty Organization (NATO) established, 1949

5

APRIL

✝ St. Vincent Ferrer (1350?–1419), priest and teacher
@ Tomb-sweeping Day, a day of cleaning tombs and participating in rites for the dead in Taiwan, Republic of China
❖ Birthday of Booker T. Washington (1856–1915), black American leader and educator

6

🖼 Birthday of Raphael (1483–1520), Italian painter
of the High Renaissance
● First modern Olympic games formally opened in Athens, Greece, 1896
❖ Matthew Henson and Commodore Robert Peary reached the North Pole, 1909
❖ The Mormon church, the Church of Jesus Christ of Latter Day Saints, founded by Joseph Smith and Oliver Crowdy, 1830

7

A P R I L

✝ St. John Baptist de la Salle (1651–1719), founder of the Christian Brothers and patron of schoolteachers [Catholic]

@ World Health Day, World Health Organization established, 1948

✎ Birthday of Gabriela Mistral (1899–1957), Chilean poet and educator, whose work for children includes *Crickets and Frogs: A Fable*

✎ Birthday of William Wordsworth (1770–1850), English poet laureate

♪ Birthday of Billie Holiday (1915–1959), blues singer

❖ No Housework Day, a day for no trash, no dishes, no making of beds or washing of laundry, and no guilt

8

✝ St. Walter (died 1095), abbot and patron saint of prisoners of war

✝ William Augustus Muhlenberg (1796–1877), American priest, hymn-writer, educator and advocate for children [Episcopal]

✝ St. Julie Billiart (1751–1816), French teacher and founder of the Sisters of Notre Dame [Catholic]

🖼 Anniversary of the death of El Greco (1541?–1614), the most influential master of Spanish painting

✡ First synagogue in America founded in New York City, 1730

❖ Hana matsuri, Buddhist feast in honor of Buddha's birth (in some countries) ❀

9 APRIL

✝ Dietrich Bonhoeffer (1906–1945), German Lutheran pastor and theologian who was executed for plotting the death of Hitler [Episcopal]
✝ William Law (1686–1761), English theological author who inspired the religious reform movements of the 18th century [Episcopal]
☨ The Civil War ended with the Treaty of Appomatox, 1865
@ Tunisia Martyr's Day
⛳ Golf Hall of Fame established, 1941
❖ First American public library opened in Peterborough, New Hampshire, 1833

10

❖ The American Society for the Prevention of Cruelty to Animals (ASPCA) founded, 1866
❖ Birthday of General William Booth (1829–1912), founder of the Salvation Army
❖ Siblings Day, to honor all brothers and sisters who are living and to memorialize those who have died

11

✞ St. Stanislaus (1030–1079), bishop, martyr and patron saint of Poland
✞ George Augustus Selwyn (1809–1878), first Anglican bishop of New Zealand [Episcopal]
@ Fast and Prayer Day in Liberia, a day of religious dedication
@ Idi Amin overthrown as dictator of the Republic of Uganda, 1979
@ Liberation of Buchenwald concentration camp, 1945

APRIL

12

☰ Bombardment of Fort Sumter, Charleston, South Carolina, beginning the Civil War, 1861
✎ Birthday of Beverly Cleary (1916 –), American children's author of books about Henry Huggins, Ramona Quimby, and others ❀
🪐 First manned space orbit around the earth, by Soviet cosmonaut Yuri Gagarin, 1961

13

✝ St. Martin I (died 655), pope and martyr

☆ Birthday of Thomas Jefferson (1743–1826), 3rd U.S. President

@ Songkran Day in Thailand, two days of tribute to monks, elders and monasteries

APRIL

14

❖ Pan American Day (est. 1931), celebrates the countries of the Western Hemisphere and the founding of the Organization of American States (OAS)

❖ Birthday of Anne Sullivan (1866–1936), American educator famous as teacher and companion to Helen Keller ❀

15

APRIL

- Income Tax returns due
- Birthday of Leonardo da Vinci (1452–1519), Italian painter, sculptor, scientist and inventor and one of the great minds of all time
- The British passenger ship *Titanic* sunk, after crashing into an iceberg, 1912

16

- Birthday of Wilbur Wright (1867–1912), American co-inventor of the airplane (with his brother, Orville)
- Queen Margrethe's birthday (1940–), observed as a holiday in Denmark, the oldest extant monarchy in Europe
- The Book-of-the-Month Club began, 1926

25

APRIL

✝ St. Mark the Evangelist, patron saint of notaries (Acts 12:12)
💡 Birthday of Gugliemo Marconi (1874–1937), Italian electrical inventor
@ Liberation Day in Italy to honor the Allied victory in World War II
@ Swaziland National Flag Day, to honor the flag and the responsibilities of citizenship
❖ Birthday of Charles Dowd (1825–1904), American educator and proponent of uniform time zones over local ones, adopted in 1883

26

🖼 Birthday of John James Audubon (1785–1851),
   American ornithologist and artist ❀
@ Explosion at Chernobyl nuclear reactor in the Ukraine, 1986
@ Union Day in Tanzania, commemorating the unification of Zanzibar and Tanganyika in 1964
💡 Birthday of Charles Richter (1900–1985), developer of the Richter scale to measure earthquakes' magnitude
❖ Birthday of Frederick Law Olmstead (1822–1903), American landscape architect and planner of Central Park in New York

27

APRIL

- ♟ Birthday of Ulysses Simpson Grant (1822–1885), Union general in the Civil War and 18th U.S. President
- 💡 Birthday of Samuel Morse (1791–1872), American inventor of the electric telegraph and the Morse code
- @ Sierra Leone Independence Day, commemorating 1961
- @ Togo Independence Day, commemorating 1960
- ❖ Anniversary of the death of Ferdinand Magellan (1480?–1521), Portuguese navigator killed while circumnavigating the globe

28

- ✝ St. Peter Chanel (1803–1841), first martyr of Oceania and its patron [Catholic]
- ♟ Birthday of James Monroe (1758–1831), 5th U.S. President
- ♟ Maryland became the 7th State, 1788
- ❖ Workers Memorial Day, in memory of workers injured or killed on their jobs

29

APRIL

✝ St. Catherine of Siena (1347–1380), mystic, teacher and patron saint of Italy
♪ Birthday of Sir Thomas Beecham (1879–1961), English conductor
@ Emperor's Birthday, honoring the birth of Emperor Hirohito (1901), a national holiday in Japan
♪ Birthday of Duke Ellington (1899–1974), Big Band leader and composer

30

✝ St. Pius V (1504–1572), who as pope was faced with implementing the Council of Trent after the Protestant Reformation [Catholic]
★ Louisiana became the 18th State, 1812
★ George Washington was inaugurated as 1st U.S. President in New York, 1789

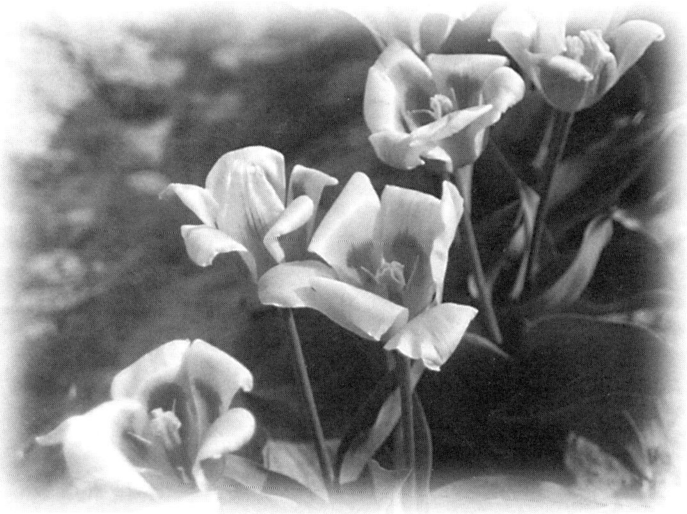

May

May is a month of remembering: of remembering spring on May Day, of remembering mothers on Mother's Day, and of remembering those who have died on Memorial Day, the last weekend of the month. We remember that the greatest things in life are given to us freely; we do nothing to "earn" the beauty of spring, the love of a mother, or the relationships that have enriched our lives.

The 1st, considered the beginning of summer in the old Celtic calendar, is a time to celebrate the flowers and colors of spring with May baskets and maypoles, as well as to celebrate workers in many European countries. This is also a time to honor Mary as the Mother of God with processions and a crowning with flowers. *All* mothers are honored on Mother's Day, the second Sunday in May. Is there something special that the mother in your life would appreciate on this day?

Though Easter Day is behind us, the season of Easter continues for 50 days. May is a month to continue the celebration of the joy of the resurrection. Ascension Thursday is always forty days after Easter. On this day we remember that the living Jesus, who had been seen by his apostles and other disciples, ascended to heaven. Though he is no longer bodily present among us, his promise to remain through the deeper presence of the Spirit is fulfilled on Pentecost. You can read about his ascent to heaven in Acts 1:1-11.

The Christian Feast of Pentecost, celebrated 50 days after Easter, often coincides with the Jewish celebration of Shavuot, the Feast of Weeks (so named because it is observed approximately 7 weeks after Passover). During Shavuot, the Jewish people give thanks for the spring harvest and for the giving of the Ten Commandments. Many devout Jews observe Shavuot by convening at the synagogue for all-night study of the Torah, which consists of the first five books of scripture. Dairy foods are traditional for this feast as reminders of the riches of the promised land and of the goodness of the Law, which is as sweet to Jews as milk and honey (Psalm 19:7-10).

On Pentecost, Christians celebrate the giving of the Spirit to every believer, empowering us to live as Christ in the world. You can read about this event in Acts 2:1-4. The rest of that chapter tells about the sermon that Peter gave to the crowd witnessing these things. His conclusion is given in verses 38-39, wherein we read that "the promise [of the Spirit] is for you, for your children, and for all who are far away, everyone whom the Lord our God calls to him." (For more on Pentecost, see the introduction to the month of June.)

This rich life of God is given to us in many ways. At this time of year, planting and tending a garden can be a powerful way to experience the energy that hope can bring as we cover small, hard seeds and wait for the wonder of new life. In this fast-paced, technological world, it is good to stay close to the earth and receive its reminders of God's goodness.

The prophet Isaiah's words are helpful now: "For as the rain and the snow come down from heaven, and do not return there until they have watered the earth, making it bring forth and sprout, giving seed to the sower and bread to the eater, so shall my word be that goes out from my mouth; it shall not return to me empty, but it shall accomplish that which I purpose, and succeed in the thing for which I sent it" (Isaiah 55:10-11).

CELEBRATING THE DAY

1 Honor an elderly neighbor on Senior Citizen's Day with a simple bouquet of flowers or a basket of fresh muffins or just a visit!

4 Many Christians are remembering St. Monica on this day. For a month in which we celebrate mothers, St. Monica is a good one to focus on. St. Monica was the mother of St. Augustine and, though she never wrote anything or did any great heroic work, she prayed for her son without fail. Because of her, we are blessed with a great theologian and Christian leader. Honor St. Monica with a special prayer for your children and a greater appreciation for the power of a mother's prayers.

5 For Cinco de Mayo you might fix your family's favorite Mexican dinner. Or, to mark the Korean Day of Swings, enjoy a picnic outdoors and go for a swing!

7 On the birthday of both Brahms and Tchaikovsky, play your favorite pieces from one or both of these composers. *The Nutcracker* is on video for those who enjoy this ballet.

9 Read some *Peter Pan* on Sir James Barrie's birthday. How do you feel about growing up, which Peter never wanted to do?

12 This is a day to remember and pray for nurses and hospitals and all the people they care for every day and throughout the night.

15 The Feast of St. Isidore is traditionally a time to plant seeds in the garden. Is this a good time to do so where you live? (If you do plant now, say a prayer that God will bless this garden with much life and beauty.) Also today on Frank Baum's birthday read some of the Wizard of Oz or some of the other, lesser-known books in the Oz series.

16 On the anniversary of the first Oscars have your own family "Oscars." What would be your categories and who would be the nominees and the winners be?

17 With older children, talk about racial segregation and other inequalities in the public school system. How do they experience or witness prejudice? What can they do to stop it?

19 Adults can read Malcolm X's autobiography or rent the movie *Malcolm X* to find out more about this influential leader.

20 Rose Hawthorne Lathrop cared for those with cancer. Is there anyone you know with cancer or recovering from it that you would like to pray for in a special way today?

22 Read your favorite Sherlock Holmes adventure on the anniversary of Sir Arthur Conan Doyle's birth.

29 Sir Edmund Hilary climbed Mt. Everest. What are your goals and how will you accomplish them?

31 On this day we remember the young, pregnant Mary visiting her older cousin, Elizabeth, who was also pregnant. Send a card to or call up a pregnant woman you know and encourage her. Who knows what her baby will turn out to do or be?

MAY

1

- ✝ St. Joseph the Worker, foster father of Jesus
- ✝ Sts. Philip and James, Apostles [Episcopal commemoration] See May 3
- ❖ May Day, which is Labor Day or International Workers' Day in 66 nations of the world
- ❖ Law Day, to honor law and its benefits to the citizen
- ❖ Senior Citizen's Day ✿
- ❖ Lei Day in Hawaii, in honor of the symbol of Hawaiian beauty and friendship

2

- ✝ St. Athanasius (295?–373), bishop of Alexandria and early champion of the truth against false teachings
- ✡ Birthday of Theodor Herzl (1860–1904), founder of modern Zionism
- ❖ Birthday of Henry Robert (1837–1923), American parliamentarian famous for *Robert's Rules of Order*

3

✝ Sts. Philip and James, Apostles [Catholic commemoration] See May 1
☮ Japanese Constitution Day, celebrating the establishment of a democratic government in 1947
☮ Polish Constitution Day, Swieto Trzeciego Majo, commemorating the first constitution for Poland, 1794

4

✝ St. Monica [Episcopal commemoration]
   See August 27 ❀
❖ Birthday of Horace Mann (1796–1859), American educator, known as the Father of the Public School System
❖ Students' Memorial Day, in memory of 4 students killed during anti-war demonstrations at Kent State University in 1970 and of students martyred elsewhere

5

M A Y

- Cinco de Mayo, a Mexican holiday celebrating the defeat of the French at the Battle of Puebla in 1867
- Birthday of Sören Kierkegaard (1813–1855), author, Danish philosopher and Christian existentialist
- Children's Day in Japan, Tango-no-sekku, honoring children
- Liberation Day in Denmark and the Netherlands, marking the end of Nazi occupation in 1945
- Day of Swings, a Korean spring holiday

6

- Martyr's Day in Lebanon, honoring the martyrs of ancient and modern times
- Shepherd's and Herdsmen's day, an old folk festival day in Bulgaria
- ❖ First stamps to prepay postage on letters issued in Great Britain, 1840
- ❖ Birthday of Sigmund Freud (1856–1939), Austrian physician and the Father of Psychoanalysis
- ❖ Birthday of Rear Admiral Robert Peary (1856–1920), American Arctic explorer

7

M A Y

♪ Birthday of Johannes Brahms (1833–1897), German classical composer ❀

✒ Birthday of Robert Browning (1812–1889), English poet, author of *The Ring and the Book*, and husband of poet Elizabeth Barrett Browning

🖼 Birthday of Sir Rabindranath Tagore (1861–1941), Hindu poet, philosopher and artist

♪ Birthday of Peter Tchaikovsky (1840–1893), Russian symphonic composer of *The Nutcracker* and other ballets ❀

@ Spring Day in Scotland

❖ American Medical Association organized, 1847

8

✝ Dame Julian of Norwich (1342–1417?), English hermit and mystic

♛ Birthday of Harry S. Truman, (1884–1972), 33rd U.S. President

@ V-E (Victory in Europe) Day, the end of World War II in Europe, 1945

@ Stork Day, traditional day for the storks' return to Denmark to repair their nests on the tops of old houses

@ Birthday of Miguel Hidalgo (1753–1811), father of Mexican Independence

❖ World Red Cross Day, on the birthday of Henri Dunant (1828–1910), Swiss philanthropist and founder of the Red Cross Society

9

M A Y

☦ St. Gregory Nazianzus [Episcopal commemoration] See January 2
⚱ Birthday of Sir James Barrie (1860–1937), Scottish writer and playwright, author of *Peter Pan* ❦
❖ The first flight over the North Pole was achieved by Commander Richard E. Byrd of the U.S. Navy and Floyd Bennet, 1926

10

☦ Blessed Damien of Molokai (1840–1889), who, while a missionary among the lepers in Hawaii, was stricken also with the disease [Catholic]
🚂 The first transcontinental railroad completed with the driving of a golden spike, 1869
❖ First Mother's Day observed in Philadelphia in 1872

11

- Minnesota became the 32nd State, 1858
- Laos Constitution Day honoring the constitution of 1947

MAY

12

- Sts. Nereus and Achilleus (first century?), Roman soldiers and martyrs
- St. Pancras of Rome (died 304?), martyr at age 14
- Birthday of Gabriel Dante Rossetti (1828–1882), English poet and Pre-Raphaelite painter
- Birthday of Florence Nightingale (1820–1910), English nurse and the founder of modern nursing
- National Hospital Day, observed since 1921 by many hospitals with special programs honoring Florence Nightingale

13

- The first permanent English settlement in America, Jamestown, Virginia, established, 1607
- Birthday of Sir Arthur Sullivan (1842–1900), British composer with William Gilbert of popular operettas

14

- St. Matthias, apostle chosen after the death of Judas (Acts 1:15-26) [Catholic commemoration] See February 24
- Kamuzu Day, a holiday in Malawi bearing the first name of the first president, Dr. Kamuzu Banda
- Paraguay Independence Day, celebrating its separation from Spain in 1811
- Skylab I, the first U.S. manned spacelab, launched in 1973 and stayed in orbit 28 days
- First American major league baseball stadium built in Brooklyn, New York, 1862

15

✝ St. Isidore the Farmer (1070–1130), patron of farmers, rural communities and Madrid, Spain ❀
✒ Birthday of L. Frank Baum (1856–1919), American writer of *The Wizard of Oz* series ❀
⚖ Peace Officers' Memorial Day

16

✝ St. Brendan (died 577 or 583), Abbot of Clonfert and an important leader of the Irish church
❖ The first movie "Oscars" were awarded in 1929 ❀

17

M A Y

- Norwegian Independence Day, marking the adoption of the constitution in 1814
- The Supreme Court banned racial segregation in the public schools, 1954
- First Kentucky Derby horse race held, 1875
- New York Stock Exchange founded, 1792

18

- St. John I (died 526), pope and martyr
- St. Eric of Sweden (died 1160), king, martyr and patron saint of Sweden
- Haitian Flag Day
- Mount St. Helens erupted, 1980
- Massachusetts became the first state to make school attendance mandatory, 1852

19

MAY

☦ St. Dunstan (910?–988), Archbishop of Canterbury and patron saint of goldsmiths, jewelers and locksmiths

@ Flag Day of the Army in Finland, honoring those who died for their country

❖ The Federated Boys' Clubs, now known as the Boys' Clubs of America, founded in 1906

❖ Birthday of Malcolm Little, known as Malcolm X (1925–1965), black Muslim leader whose *Autobiography* was widely influential ✿

20

☦ St. Bernardine of Siena (1380–1444), preacher and Franciscan leader, patron saint of publicity agents

☦ Birthday of Rose Hawthorne Lathrop (1851–1926), American nun who dedicated her life to the care of those incurably ill with cancer [Catholic] ✿

☦ Alcuin (730?–804), abbot and scholar at the time of Charlemagne

☦ Birthday of Franz Jagerstatter (1907–1943), German conscientious objector [Catholic]

@ Cuban Independence Day, commemorating its break with Spain in 1902

@ Independence Day in Saudi Arabia since 1927

21
M A Y

- Birthday of Albrecht Dürer (1471–1528), German painter and printmaker
- ❖ American Charles Lindbergh arrived in Paris, having completed the first solo transatlantic flight, 1927
- ❖ The American Red Cross was founded by Clara Barton, 1881

22

- Birthday of Sir Arthur Conan Doyle (1859–1930), British novelist and creator of Sherlock Holmes
- ♪ Birthday of Richard Wagner (1813–1883), German operatic composer
- @ Sri Lanka Republic Day, whose constitution was ratified in 1972
- ❖ The Associated Press organized, 1900
- ❖ National Maritime Day, celebrating the first steamboat crossing of the Atlantic Ocean, 1819

23 M A Y

☗ South Carolina became the 8th State, 1788

⚗ Birthday of Carolus Linnaeus (1707–1778), Swedish naturalist who developed new methods of classifying plants

℮ The German Federal Republic (West Germany) established, 1949

℮ Jamaican Labour Day, saluting the Jamaican worker

24

☦ Jackson Kemper (1789–1870), first missionary bishop in the United States and a founder of Nashotah House [Episcopal]

℮ Bulgarian Day of Slavonic Letters, a tribute to Bulgarian culture, education and communications

℮ Victoria Day, celebrated in England and other countries to commemorate the birthday of Queen Victoria (1819–1901)

25

M A Y

✝ St. Bede the Venerable (672?–735), British monk, scholar and historian
✝ St. Gregory VII (1020–1085), pope and reformer
✝ St. Mary Magdalene de Pazzi (1566–1607), Italian nun and mystic [Catholic]
⚱ Birthday of Ralph Waldo Emerson (1803–1882), American essayist, poet and lecturer
@ Revolución de Mayo, anniversary of the 1810 revolution in Argentina
@ Jordan Independence Day and Arab Renaissance Day, honoring the treaty of 1946, giving Jordan autonomy and a monarchy

26

✝ St. Philip Neri (1515–1595), active layman and founder of the Congregation of the Oratory [Catholic]
✝ St. Augustine of Canterbury [Episcopal commemoration] See May 27
@ Guyana Independence Day, honoring the agreement of 1966

MAY

27

✝ St. Augustine of Canterbury (died 605?), missionary and apostle to the English [Catholic commemoration] See May 26

⚗ Birthday of Rachel Carson (1907–1964), American biologist and environmentalist

@ Afghanistan Independence Day, honoring sovereignty achieved in 1919

✒ Birthday of Julia Ward Howe (1819–1910), American author, social reformer and author of "The Battle Hymn of the Republic"

@ Children's Day in Nigeria, honoring kids from more than 100 tribes

28

✝ St. Bernard of Mountjoux (died c. 1081) who traveled through the Alps caring for travellers, patron saint of mountain climbers

@ Puerto Rican Memorial Day

● Birthday of Jim Thorpe (1888–1953), Native American all-around athlete, who excelled in football, track and field and baseball

29

MAY

⚱ Birthday of Gilbert Keith (G.K.) Chesterton (1874–1936), English journalist, novelist, poet and critic, author of the Father Brown detective novels

♚ Birthday of John Fitzgerald Kennedy (1917–1963), 35th U.S. President

♚ Rhode Island became the 13th State, 1790

♚ Wisconsin became the 30th State, 1848

❖ Sir Edmund Hillary of New Zealand and Tenzing Norkay of Nepal, the first to reach the summit of Mt. Everest, the world's highest peak, in 1953

30

✝ St. Joan of Arc (1412–1431), martyr and patron saint of France in honor of her obedient response to God's call to repel the English armies

♚ Lincoln Memorial dedicated, 1922

♚ First Memorial Day observed, 1868, when two women placed flowers on the graves of both Union and Confederate soldiers in Mississippi

31

MAY

✝ Feast of the Visitation of Mary to Elizabeth (Luke 1:39–56) ❀

✒ Birthday of Walt Whitman (1819–1892), American poet, popular for his collection, *Leaves of Grass*

🌐 South Africa Republic Day or Union Day, honoring the unification of the South African colonies in 1910 and the republic established in 1961

JUNE

June is a month of graduations and weddings, when we shed the coolness of spring and bid goodbye to school. It's time to bask in the longest days of the year in the Northern Hemisphere and gear up for warm evenings and summer memories.

Because this is a season of graduation, now is a good time to create a simple ritual for your family to honor the completion of another year of school. Whether your child is finishing 3rd grade or college, celebrate with a flourish. Acknowledge the learning that has taken place and the spiritual, physical and mental growth of the last year. Review some of the achievements and struggles your child has experienced over the last year. Encourage your child to make goals for next year.

Pentecost usually occurs in late May or early June. (See the introduction to the month of May.) But, like Easter, the celebration is more than a day; it is a season of growing in understanding the glory of the giving of the Spirit. Now is the time to welcome the Spirit into our own midst, shaking us up as only a strong wind can do and setting us on fire to *live* Jesus' message of love, not just to *talk* about it. And so we pray: "Come, Holy Spirit, fill the hearts of your faithful and kindle in them the fire of your love. Send forth your Spirit and they shall be created, and you will renew the faith of the earth."

At Pentecost, the disciples spoke in many languages, proclaiming the gospel to all people. In Christ, the story of Babel, a story about the break in human communication (Genesis 11:1-9), is reversed. The gospel can overcome our inability to communicate with each other. This is a time to pray for that gift in our own homes.

There are many ways to celebrate this season. Make Pentecost placemats with a dove descending upon a picture of your family and cover them with self-stick clear plastic. Make a mobile with a dove for the Holy Spirit and on the seven flames below it the seven gifts of the Holy Spirit: wisdom, understanding, counsel, strength, knowledge, piety and the fear of the Lord (Isaiah 11:2-3). Talk about how those gifts are present in your family and the people you know.

On or near the 21st of the month, we enjoy the summer solstice, the longest day and shortest night of the year for the Northern Hemisphere. The Feast of the Birth of John the Baptist, the forerunner of Jesus Christ, is on June 24th, which used to be the solstice in a former calendar. This was placed so that it fell directly opposite to the birth of Jesus in the cycle of the year. The night before John the Baptist's birth, Midsummer Night's Eve on the 23rd, has been a time of rejoicing since pre-Christian times, often involving night fires celebrating the light of the sun.

Father's Day is observed on the third Sunday of the month as a day to appreciate and thank those men in our lives who have been an important presence and have shown both their strength and their tenderness in countless ways. Perhaps even more than mothers we have stereotypes of what a good dad should look like; we need to acknowledge that there are *many* ways to be a loving father.

For families with children, the myth of those "long, lazy summer days" is just that...a myth. June tends to fly by so quickly. Slow it down just a bit. You don't need to do everything. Relish the warmth and remember what's important.

CELEBRATING THE DAY

2 This is the anniversary of the first circus tour of P.T. Barnum. Have you ever been to the circus? If you have, what did you like? What didn't you like? If you were in the circus, what would you like to do?

3 Today in Japan many remember their broken dolls. What happens or happened to your broken toys? Tell the stories.

6 Have you ever been to a drive-in theater? Are there any left in your area? Pick a warm evening and pack up the family for a drive-in adventure. Also today we remember our nation's shameful treatment of our Japanese Americans. Talk with your children about the human capacity for fear and how it contaminates our relationships with prejudice and intolerance. It's easy to point the finger at the "bad Nazis," but many of us, too, have been guilty of gross bigotry toward native Americans, black Americans, Japanese Americans and others.

9 Oklahoma honors its senior citizens today. Who are the older people in your life? Are there some ways you could tell them today how special they are and perhaps listen to the stories of some of their experiences?

10 Maurice Sendak is a renowned children's illustrator and author. Check out a copy of his book, *Where the Wild Things Are*, or another of his popular books.

12 Middle school-aged young people on up would benefit from reading *The Diary of Anne Frank* if they haven't already read it. Younger children would enjoy some of *Heidi*, either in book or movie form. Today is also an important day for the sport of baseball. Have you watched, gone to or played a game of baseball lately? What's your favorite position, player and team?

14 How many flags of other countries can you identify? Flags are important symbols of countries and all that they stand for. Do you have a flag that you could display today?

24 Read about John the Baptist's unusual birth in Luke 1:5-25, 57-80. He was destined for a unique career (Matthew 3:1-6) as the forerunner of Jesus Christ. Because of his role as a prophet, he shunned some of the normal customs of daily life. You won't probably want to eat locusts and wild honey, which was part of his diet, but you could remember him today by making mock locusts with chow mein noodles drizzled with honey.

26 A silly thought: if the toothbrush had not been invented, what would we use to keep our teeth clean?

27 Helen Keller's life is an amazing story of triumph over several disabilities. Find a story of her life at your local library. Whom do you know with a disability? How do they live with it? Talk about how life might different without sight or hearing or the ability to walk or do things for yourself.

JUNE

1

✝ St. Justin (died 165), martyr and apologist, patron of philosophers

✝ Birthday of Jacques Marquette (1637–1675), French Jesuit missionary on the upper Mississippi [Catholic]

★ Kentucky became the 15th State, 1792

★ Tennessee became the 16th State, 1796

@ Children's Day in both the People's Republic of China and Zimbabwe

@ Tunisia Constitution Day, commemorating its promulgation, 1959

❖ Birthday of Brigham Young (1801–1877), American Mormon leader

2

✝ Sts. Marcellinus and Peter (died 304), martyrs

✝ The Martyrs of Lyons (died 177), early witnesses to their faith

@ Italian National Day, celebrating the republic established by referendum in 1946

@ Seaman's Day, celebrated in Iceland honoring sailors and fishermen

❖ P.T. Barnum's circus began the first U.S. tour in 1835

❖ Elizabeth II crowned Queen of England, 1953

3

JUNE

✝ St. Charles Lwanga and companions (died 1886), 22 Ugandan young men who died for their faith
☆ Birthday of Jefferson Davis (1808–1889), president of the Confederacy
@ Memorial to Broken Dolls Day, a Buddhist ceremony in Japan for little girls and their mothers to bring broken dolls to a priest ❀

4

@ Government troops opened fire on Chinese students in Tiananmen Square in Beijing after more than a month of protests, 1989

5

J U N E

✝ St. Boniface (672?–754), bishop, martyr and patron of Germany
❦ World Environment Day, to reaffirm the worldwide need for the preservation of the environment
❦ Denmark Constitution Day, marking its signing in 1849 and its revision in 1953
❦ Six-Day War between Israel and Egypt, Syria and Jordan began, 1967
🪐 Birthday of John Couch Adams (1819–1892), English astronomer who first observed the planet Neptune

6

✝ St. Norbert (1080?–1134), bishop and founder of a religious community
❦ Constitution and Flag Day in Sweden, commemorating its adoption in 1809 and Gustavus I ascending the throne in 1523
❖ D-Day, Allied forces invaded the coast of Normandy and Nazi-held western Europe, 1944
❖ The world's first drive-in theater opened in Camden, New Jersey in 1933 ❀
❖ Evacuation of Japanese Americans into "relocation" camps completed, 1942 ❀

JUNE

7

- Birthday of Paul Gaugin (1848–1903), French painter
- Birthday of Gwendolyn Brooks (1917–), American poet and author, recipient of the Pulitzer Prize for poetry in 1950
- Birthday of Nikki Giovanni (1943–), American poet
- Birthday of Sir James Simpson (1811–1870), Scottish obstetrician and developer of anesthesia
- ❖ Anniversary of the death of Seattle (1786?-1866), chief and peaceful leader of the Duwamish (Northwest) Native American tribes

8

- ❖ Birthday of Frank Lloyd Wright (1867–1959), American architect
- ❖ Anniversary of the death of Mohammed (570?–632), founder of Islam

9

JUNE

✝ St. Ephrem (306?–373), Syrian deacon and defender of the faith [Catholic commemoration] See June 10
✝ St. Columba (521?–597), Irish scholar and abbot of Iona
♪ Birthday of John Howard Payne (1791–1852), American songwriter and composer of "Home Sweet Home"
❖ Senior Citizens' Day in Oklahoma, to honor older Americans and their contributions to society ❀

10

✝ St. Ephrem of Edessa [Episcopal commemoration]
  See June 9
✉ Camões Memorial Day in Portugal, commemorating the death of Luiz Vaz de Camões, immortal Portuguese poet, in 1580
📖 Maurice Sendak (1928–), American illustrator and author of children's books ❀
❖ Alcoholics Anonymous founded in 1935 by William G. Wilson and Dr. Robert Smith

11

JUNE

✝ St. Barnabas, apostle and companion of St. Paul (Acts 4:36-37, 11:20-26)
✒ Birthday of Ben Jonson (1572–1637), Elizabethan playwright and poet
✒ Birthday of Gerard Manley Hopkins (1844–1889), English Jesuit poet
❖ Kamehameha Day in Hawaii, commemorating the victories of King Kamehameha I, who unified the islands in the 18th century

12

✒ Birthday of Anne Frank (1929–1945), German-Dutch Jewish girl whose diary describing hiding from the Nazis is widely read ✿
★ Birthday of George Bush (1924–), 41st U.S. President
★ Anniversary of the death of Medgar Evans (1963) by assassination, black American civil rights leader
@ Helsinki Day in Finland to celebrate the founding of that city in 1550
@ Independence Day in the Philippines to celebrate independence from Spain in 1898
● Baseball invented in 1839, and the Baseball Hall of Fame opened in Cooperstown, New York in 1939 ✿
✒ Birthday of Johanna Spyri (1827–1901), Swiss author of *Heidi* ✿

13

JUNE

✝ St. Anthony of Padua (1195–1231), Franciscan preacher and scholar, patron saint of the illiterate and advocate of the poor
✒ William Butler Yeats (1865–1939), Irish poet and dramatist and 1923 recipient of the Nobel Prize in Literature

14

✝ St. Basil the Great [Episcopal commemoration]
   See January 2
☆ Flag Day, to commemorate the adoption of the Stars and Stripes by the Continental Congress in 1777 ❀
✒ Birthday of Harriet Beecher Stowe (1811–1896), American novelist and author of *Uncle Tom's Cabin*
@ Mother's Day in Afghanistan

15

JUNE

✞ Evelyn Underhill (1875–1941), Anglican author who wrote on mysticism and prayer [Episcopal]

★ Arkansas became the 25th State, 1836

♪ Birthday of Edvard Grieg (1843–1907), Norwegian composer

★ The Oregon Treaty, fixing the northwest boundary of the States at the 49th parallel to the Pacific Ocean, signed with Great Britain in 1846

@ Farmer's Day in Korea, a day for transplanting rice seedlings

❖ Magna Charta, document on which English law is based, signed in 1215

16

✞ Joseph Butler (1692–1752), Anglican bishop and apologist [Episcopal]

☄ The first woman in space, Soviet cosmonaut Valentina Tereshkova, 1963

@ The Soweto Uprising in South Africa, during which 575 blacks were killed, 1976

17

JUNE

✝ Birthday of John Wesley (1703–1791), English evangelist and founder of Methodism [Episcopal]
♖ The Battle of Bunker Hill, Revolutionary War, 1775
♖ Watergate break-in at the Democratic National Headquarters, a political scandal, 1972
✒ Birthday of James Weldon Johnson (1871–1938), American poet and lawyer
@ National Day in Iceland, remembering the republic reestablished in 1944 and the birth of Jon Sigurdson (1811), its outstanding leader

18

✝ Bernard Mizeki (1861?–1896), Anglican catechist and martyr in Rhodesia [Episcopal]
@ The Battle of Waterloo lost by Napoleon, 1815
@ Evacuation Day in the United Arab Republic (Egypt), when the last of the foreign troops left, 1956

19

JUNE

† St. Romuald (950?–1027), abbot and founder of religious communities
✒ Birthday of Blaise Pascal (1623–1662), French philosopher, mathematician, author and scientist
@ Independence Day in Kuwait, begun in 1961
★ Juneteenth celebration, honoring the emancipation of slaves, proclaimed in Texas on this date, 1865
❖ The first Father's Day was observed in 1910 in Spokane, Washington

20

★ West Virginia became the 25th State, 1863
@ Argentina Flag Day
@ Senegal Independence Day, celebrated by the former French colony since 1960

21

JUNE

✝ St. Aloysius Gonzaga (1568–1591), Jesuit and patron saint of youth [Catholic]

★ New Hampshire became the 9th State, 1788

❖ Birthday of Reinhold Niebuhr (1892–1971), American theologian and author of the prayer, "God, grant me the serenity to accept the things I cannot change, courage to change the things I can, and the wisdom to know the difference"

22

✝ St. Paulinus of Nola (354?–431), an early bishop

✝ St. John Fisher (1469–1535), English scholar, bishop and martyr [Catholic]

✝ St. Thomas More (1478–1535), English lawyer, scholar and martyr [Catholic]

✝ St. Alban (died 304?), traditionally the first British martyr

★ The voting age changed from 21 to 18 in 1970

@ Haitian President's Day

@ Schoolteachers' Day in El Salvador

23

- Midsummer Eve, or Saint John's Eve, the opening of major holiday festivities in Finland, Latvia and the Scandinavian countries to celebrate the beginning of summer
- Luxembourg National Day, celebrating the Grand Duke's birthday

24

- ✝ The Birth of John the Baptist, Jesus' cousin and prophet and patron saint of missionaries and tailors ❀
- San Juan Day in Puerto Rico
- Bannockburn Day in Scotland, in honor of Robert Bruce expelling the English in 1314
- Day of the Indian, or Dia del Indio, celebrated in Peru and other Latin American countries to preserve and enjoy native culture

25

★ Virginia became the 10th State, 1788

★ "Custer's Last Stand," at the Battle of Little Big Horn, Montana, when he and his forces were wiped out by Native warriors, 1876

26

Birthday of Pearl S. Buck (1892–1973), American author of books about China, awarded the Pulitzer Prize in 1932 for *The Good Earth*

Independence Day for Somalia and Madagascar, 1960

The United Nations Charter was ratified in San Francisco, 1945

❖ The toothbrush was invented, 1498 ❀

❖ The Saint Lawrence Seaway was officially dedicated, 1959

JUNE

27

✝ St. Cyril of Alexandria (376?–444), bishop and apologist
✝ Birthday of Pierre Toussaint (1766–1853), a black hairdresser who practiced charity toward all in early New York City [Catholic]
⚱ Birthday of Helen Keller (1880–1968), the most accomplished blind woman of the 20th century ❀

28

✝ St. Irenaeus (130?–220), early bishop and teacher
⚱ Birthday of Jean-Jacques Rousseau (1712–1778), French philosopher and author
🖼 Birthday of Peter Paul Rubens (1577–1640), Flemish artist
@ Treaty of Versailles signed 1919, ending World War I
@ Mnarja Folk Festival Day in Malta with customs re-created from the Middle Ages

JUNE

29

✟ Sts. Peter and Paul, apostles and key figures in the Church's beginnings
❖ Birthday of William Mayo (1861–1939), American surgeon and co-founder, with his brother Charles, of the Mayo Clinic

30

✟ The First Martyrs of the Church of Rome (died 64), "a great multitude" of Christians who were put to death under Nero, blamed for a fire in Rome
☉ Revolution Day in Guatemala, celebrating the agrarian reforms of 1871
☉ Zaire Independence Day, commemorating its independence in 1960

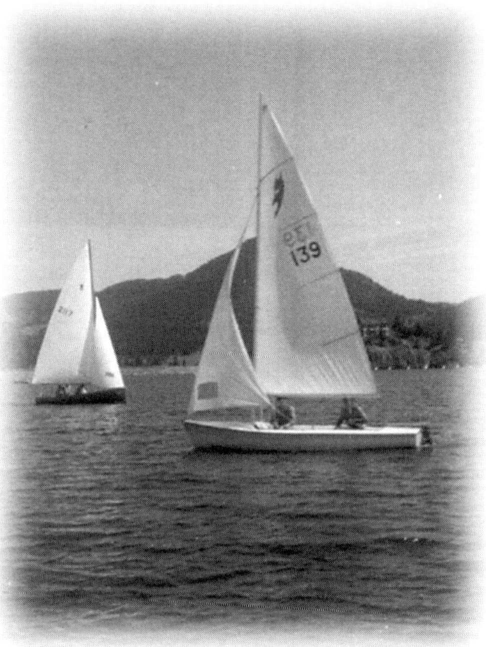
139

JULY

July is a month of fireworks and hot weather, of travel and enjoying life. The days are long, the nights are short, and everyone looks for ways to stay cool.

The 3rd of July begins the Dog Days of summer, traditionally the hottest five weeks of the year, which continue through the 11th of August. They are so named for Sirius, the Dog Star, the brightest star in the sky, which becomes visible on the horizon at dawn during this season.

What does your family do to take advantage of this weather? Do you camp or go to the beach or the lake? Do you take time to see new places in this amazing world of ours? Is there someone who helps record your trips with pictures or a travel journal? Do you say a prayer for safety and a sense of wonder as you begin your trip and a prayer of thanksgiving as you return home?

British author G.K. Chesterton once observed that the purpose of all trips is to come home—but to do so with new eyes and a new heart. Has that happened to your family? How? On your next trip, try bringing along a portable tape recorder with a blank tape and interview one another or tell a progressive story about the trip. It will be fun to listen to years from now. What is the most memorable vacation for each member of your family? Why? This would be a good time of year to get out photos, slides or videos from other years and remember those times together.

A focus on the weather is certainly nothing new this time of year. Old St. Swithin's Day, a former feast day on July 15th, was a traditional day for weather forecasting. "St. Swithin's Day, if thou dost rain, for 40 days it will remain; St. Swithin's Day, if thou be fair, for 40 days 'twill rain nae mair [no more]."

Tisha Be'Av, the ninth day of the Jewish month of Av, usually falls in late July or early August. The day is preceded by three weeks of mourning, which recall the weeks after the Romans invaded Jerusalem in A.D. 70. Tisha Be'Av commemorates the day that the Romans destroyed the Temple *and* the day that the Babylonians destroyed the first Temple (586 B.C.), which happened on the same day. It is a full fast day (the only other one being Yom Kippur), and observers gather in the synagogue, sit on the floor, and read together the Book of Lamentations.

As Christians, we continue the season of spiritual growth that began with Pentecost. The scripture readings from the lectionary often focus on God's provision, both physical and spiritual. With all the abundance around us during this verdant month, it is not hard to remember the Providence that makes life possible.

Scripture reminds us that our inner being is also growing under God's watchful eye: "The righteous flourish like the palm tree, and grow like a cedar in Lebanon. They are planted in the house of the Lord; they flourish in the courts of our God. In old age they still produce fruit; they are always green and full of sap, showing that the Lord is upright" (Psalm 92:12-15).

CELEBRATING THE DAY

1 This is the anniversary of the first U.S. stamps. Is anyone in your family a stamp collector or do you know anyone who is? It can be a fascinating and fun hobby.

3 Read about St. Thomas in John 20:24-29. Give thanks for Thomas's persistence and pray for each family member's journey of faith.

4 What does your family do to celebrate Independence Day? Does it involve a picnic and watching fireworks? This is also Stephen Foster's birthday. Do you know any of his songs, such as "My Old Kentucky Home" or "Camptown Races" or "Old Folks at Home"?

6 What is it about Beatrix Potter's gentle illustrations and children's stories that are so appealing? Try reading *The Tale of Peter Rabbit* or another of your favorites together tonight.

7 Today is a Japanese Star Festival. How many stars and constellations can you recognize? Watch the stars tonight.

8 The passport is the symbol for foreign travel. Do you have a passport? Have you traveled to other countries or do you know someone who has? Have you been to Washington, D.C. (the **16**th) or Disneyland (the **17**th) or Disney World? What has been your favorite trip? Invite young children to make their own passports with construction paper and crayons. They should draw their picture on one page, fill in important information about themselves, and sketch entry certification to countries they would like to visit, real or fanciful.

11 If you haven't already done so, treat your family to *Charlotte's Web* or *Trumpet of the Swan* or *Stuart Little* by E.B. White.

12 George Eastman's birthday is a time to celebrate cameras and photography. Who takes most of the pictures in your family? Perhaps this is a good time to pull out the family albums or boxes of pictures and remember some good times.

15 Can anyone in your family recite "The Night Before Christmas" from memory—in July?

18 Today we honor Nelson Mandela, South Africa's first black president. For 28 years he languished in prison for his political beliefs; now he leads his country into a new era of freedom and equality. Many others around the world suffer for their political leadership. Write Amnesty International, 322 8th Avenue, New York, NY 10001 for information on political prisoners around the world today.

20 What would you have said and done if *you* were the first on the moon?

23 Celebrate the invention of the ice cream cone by having one!

29 Remember St. Martha by reading about her in John 11. In the midst of her grief over her brother's death, she makes a great declaration of faith: "Lord, I believe that you are the Messiah, the Son of God, the one coming into the world." What makes it possible to believe even when things are at their worst?

31 In honor of the first U.S. patent ever issued, invent something! If you could create some kind of machine or discover some formula for a product, what would it be? Let each family member come up with his or her most fantastic idea, and then "patent" it.

JULY

1

✟ St. Junipero Serra (1713–1784), Franciscan missionary among the Native Americans in early California [Catholic]

@ Independence Day in Rwanda and Burundi, since 1962

@ Dominion Day or Canada Day, remembering the confederation of 1867

@ Half-Year Day, a holiday in Hong Kong

★ First U.S. postage stamps issued, 1847

@ Republic Day in Somalia and Ghana, celebrated since 1960

❖ The Gideons were established to distribute the Bible to travelers, 1899

2

✟ Birthday of Thomas Cranmer (1489–1556), Archbishop of Canterbury and chief author of *The Book of Common Prayer* [Episcopal]

★ Birthday of Thurgood Marshall (1908–1995), first black Supreme Court justice

★ Passage of Civil Rights Act, protecting every citizen's rights, 1964

JULY

3

- St. Thomas, the apostle who doubted and later believed, patron of the East Indies and India and of architects and builders [Catholic commemoration] See December 21
- Birthday of Franz Kafka (1883–1924), Austrian novelist and short-story writer
- Idaho became the 43rd State, 1890
- Algerian Independence Day, marking the end of 130 years of French rule in 1962

4

- St. Elizabeth of Portugal (1271–1336), queen and peacemaker
- Independence Day, honoring the Declaration of Independence, which was signed in 1776
- Birthday of Calvin Coolidge (1872–1933), 30th U.S. President
- Birthday of Stephen Foster (1826–1864), American pre-Civil War composer of songs
- Birthday of Nathaniel Hawthorne (1804–1864), American novelist, best known for *The Scarlet Letter*
- Birthday of Giuseppi Garibaldi (1807–1882), Italian national leader

5

✝ St. Anthony Zaccaria (1502–1539), Italian priest and reformer [Catholic]
@ Venezuela declared independence from Spain in 1811, the first South American country to do so
❖ Birthday of Phineas T. Barnum (1810–1891), American circus showman

6

✝ St. Maria Goretti (1890–1902), Italian martyr and model of purity [Catholic]
✝ Anniversary of the death of Jan Huss (1374–1415), Czech religious reformer burned at the stake
⚓ Birthday of John Paul Jones (1747–1792), naval hero of the American Revolution
@ Malawi Republic Day, remembering independence since 1965
♁ Birthday of Beatrix Potter (1886–1943), English author and illustrator of children's stories, notably *The Tale of Peter Rabbit* ❀

7

J U L Y

- The Star Festival, or Tanabata, a Japanese festival based on a legend about two star-lovers who meet only on the 7th night of the 7th month
- Birthday of Marc Chagall (1887–1985), Russian-born artist and illustrator

8

- The first passport issued for foreign travel, 1796
- The Liberty Bell cracked in 1835
- Birthday of John D. Rockefeller (1839–1937), American industrialist and philanthropist

JULY

9

- Birthday of Elias Howe (1819–1867), American inventor of the sewing machine
- Argentina Independence Day since 1816
- Fourteenth Amendment ratified (1868), guaranteeing citizenship to blacks

10

- Birthday of John Calvin (1509–1564), Protestant theologian and reformer
- Wyoming became the 44th State, 1890
- Independence Day in the Bahama Islands since 1973
- Birthday of Toyohiko Kagawa (1888–1960), Japanese social reformer and labor leader
- Birthday of Mary McLeod Bethune (1875–1955), educator of black Americans

JULY

11

† St. Benedict (480?–543), founder of the Benedictine order and Western monastic life

☆ Birthday of John Quincy Adams (1767–1848), 6th U.S. President

✒ Birthday of Elwyn Brooks (E.B.) White (1899–1985), American essayist, author of *Charlotte's Web* and other children's books ❀

12

💡 Birthday of George Eastman (1854–1932), American inventor of cameras and camera equipment ❀

✒ Birthday of Henry David Thoreau (1817–1862), American naturalist and author of *Walden, or Life in the Woods*

@ Orangeman's Day or Orange Day, the anniversary of the Battle of the Boyne in 1690, celebrated in Northern Ireland

💡 Birthday of R. Buckminster Fuller (1895–1983), American inventor and engineer who designed the geodesic dome

13

JULY

✝ St. Henry (972–1024), German king and Roman emperor

❧ Night Watch, or La Retraite aux Flambeaux, the eve of Bastille Day in France

14

✝ Blessed Kateri Tekakwitha (1656–1680), Native American convert, called the "Lily of the Mohawks" [Catholic]

❧ Bastille Day in France, commemorating the storming of the Bastille prison in 1789 and the release of political prisoners

⚱ Birthday of Gerald Ford (1913–), 38th U.S. President

🖼 Birthday of James Whistler (1834–1903), American artist and wit

⚗ Birthday of Florence Bascom (1863–1945), American geologist and first woman to receive a Ph.D. from any American university

❖ Birthday of Emmeline Pankhurst (1858–1928), English militant suffragist

15

JULY

- St. Bonaventure (1221–1274), Franciscan theologian and teacher
- Birthday of Clement Clarke Moore (1779–1863), American scholar and poet, author of "The Night Before Christmas," originally *A Visit from Saint Nicholas*
- Birthday of Rembrandt van Rijn (1606–1669), Dutch painter and etcher
- Japanese Obon Festival, or Feast of Lanterns, begins, a tribute to deceased ancestors

16

- Feast of Our Lady of Mount Carmel, patron saint of fishermen, a special feast for the Carmelite order [Catholic]
- District of Columbia established as the permanent capital, 1790
- La Paz founded as the capital of Bolivia, 1548
- First parking meter installed, in Oklahoma City, in 1935
- Birthday of Mary Baker Eddy (1821–1910), founder of Christian Science

17

JULY

✞ William White (1747–1836), early American bishop, theologian and organizer of the Episcopal Church [Episcopal]

@ Constitution Day in South Korea, celebrating its adoption in 1963

❖ Birthday of John Jacob Astor (1763–1848), German-American fur trader and capitalist

❖ Disneyland (California) opened, 1955

18

✞ St. Camillus de Lellis (1550–1614), patron saint of the sick and of nurses [Catholic]

✒ Birthday of William Makepeace Thackeray (1811–1863), English novelist and author of *Vanity Fair*

@ Labor Day in Spain

@ Constitution adopted in Uruguay, 1951

❖ Birthday of Nelson Mandela (1918 –), South African leader for racial equality, jailed for 28 years and released in 1990

JULY

19

✝ St. Macrina (340–379), monk, theologian, teacher and the sister of St. Basil and St. Gregory the Great

☥ First Women's Rights Convention held in Seneca Falls, New York, 1848, organized by Elizabeth Cady Stanton and others

❖ Birthday of Charles Mayo (1865–1939), American co-founder with his brother, William, of the Mayo Clinic

℮ Laos achieved full independence from France, 1954

20

The first manned landing on the moon by Neil Armstrong and "Buzz" Aldrin in the Apollo II, 1969

Birthday of Francesco Petrarch (1304–1374), Italian lyric poet and scholar, a major figure in the Renaissance

21

JULY

✟ St. Lawrence of Brindisi (1559–1619), Capuchin scholar and administrator [Catholic]

★ Veteran's Administration established, 1930

✍ Birthday of Ernest Hemingway (1899–1961), American novelist, short story writer and world traveler

@ Belgium became independent of the Netherlands, 1831

@ Liberation Day in Guam when the Army freed it from the Japanese, 1944

22

✟ Mary Magdalene, a close friend of Jesus and first witness to the risen Lord (John 20:10-18)

✍ Birthday of Stephen Vincent Benet (1898–1943), American poet and novelist

✍ Birthday of Emma Lazarus (1849–1887), American poet who wrote the lines engraved on the Statue of Liberty, "Give me your tired, your poor"

@ Polish National Liberation Day in honor of the end of the war in 1944 and the constitution in 1952

23

✝ St. Bridget (1303?–1373), Swedish mystic, mother and founder of a religious community
🕮 Day of the Republic in Egypt and Libya since 1952
🕮 Oman National Day
❖ The ice cream cone was invented by Italo Marchioni at the World's Fair in St. Louis, Missouri, 1903

JULY

24

✝ Thomas à Kempis (1380?–1471), medieval spiritual author of *The Imitation of Christ*
🕮 Birthday of Simon Bolivar (1783–1830), "The Liberator," Venezuelan soldier and South American liberator
❖ Birthday of Amelia Earhart (1898–1937), American aviatrix and the first woman to fly solo across the Atlantic Ocean

25

✝ St. James, the apostle and brother of John, first apostle to be martyred (Acts 12:1-2)

⚱ Puerto Rico became a commonwealth, 1952

@ Tunisia established as a republic, 1957

@ Netherlands Independence Day, honoring 19th-century events ensuring the constitutional monarchy of the country today

❖ Louise Brown of Oldham, England, the first "test tube baby," born 1978

26

✝ Sts. Joachim and Anne, parents of Mary, "grandparents of God" (Saint Anne is the patron saint of Canada.)

⚱ New York became the 11th State, 1788

✒ Birthday of George Bernard Shaw (1856–1950), Irish-English playwright

@ Cuban revolution under Fidel Castro overthrew the Batista military dictatorship, 1953

@ Liberia established as a republic and a place to send freed "Negroes" from the United States, 1847

27

† William Reed Huntington (died 1909), American priest and advocate of Christian unity [Episcopal]

☗ The Korean War ended with the signing of an armistice, 1953

28

@ Somers Day in Bermuda in honor of its settlement by Admiral Sir George Somers in 1609

@ Peru declared independence from Spain in 1821

29

JULY

✝ St. Martha, friend of Jesus with her sister Mary and her brother Lazarus, patron saint of housewives, cooks, innkeepers and laundresses ✿

✝ St. Olaf (995–1030), King of Norway and martyr; a major holiday in Norway

@ The International Atomic Agency begun to ensure peaceful benefits of atomic research to peoples throughout the world, 1957

30

✝ St. Peter Chrysologus (406–450?), preacher and teacher

✝ William Wilberforce (1759–1833), Anglican layman and politician, instrumental in abolishing slavery in Great Britain [Episcopal]

✎ Birthday of Emily Bronte (1818–1848), English author famous for *Wuthering Heights*

💡 Birthday of Henry Ford (1863–1947), American inventor, automobile manufacturer and philanthropist

♪ The "Marseillaise," the national anthem of France, first sung in 1792

JULY

31

✝ St. Ignatius of Loyola (1491–1556), founder of the Jesuits and author of the *Spiritual Exercises*, patron saint of retreats and retreatants

✝ Joseph of Arimathea [Episcopal commemoration] See March 17

💡 Birthday of John Ericsson (1803–1889), American inventor of the screw propeller and pioneer in modern naval construction

💡 The first U.S. patent ever issued was granted to Samuel Hopkins for processing potash, a substance used in the manufacture of soap and glass, 1790

AUGUST

In August we begin to wrap up the summer. Vacations end; school begins; the crickets sing loud and long in the lingering twilight. This is lush time when we begin to look forward to the coolness of fall and the riches of the harvest.

Lammastide is an old name for the first two weeks of August. The word *lammas* apparently comes from "loaf Mass," because our ancestors would carry loaves of bread made from the first grains of the newly harvested wheat to the churches to be blessed. This is a very old custom, one which in the Judeo-Christian tradition goes all the way back to the Israelites who would bring their first fruits to the temple as an offering, as a reminder of all God's provision, and as a prayer for God's continued blessing. (Read about this ancient ritual in Deuteronomy 26:1-15.) The Eastern Church still observes a two-week fast during Lammastide in preparation for the Feast of Mary's Assumption on the 15th.

On the 6th of August we celebrate the Feast of the Transfiguration of the Lord. Jesus is revealed in his true glory as recorded in Matthew 17:1-8, Mark 9:2-8 or Luke 9:28-36. At this time when the earth is being clothed in its autumn harvest glory, we remember Jesus' majesty and splendor, often hidden from us in his humble servanthood.

The Jewish month of Ellul usually begins during this time. As the last month of the Jewish calendar, this is a time for renewal and prayer in anticipation of the New Year, which begins next month on Rosh Hashana. On every day but the Sabbath and the last day of Ellul, the shofar (twisted ram's horn) is sounded to remind the people of God's goodness to Abraham, especially revealed when the human sacrifice of Isaac was replaced with a ram. The blowing of the shofar can also be seen as a "wake-up call" to reexamine our lives and how we use our time.

In a sense, the Assumption of Mary is a harvest festival, celebrating the completion and fulfillment of the life of Jesus' mother and recognizing her entrance into glory. Flowers and fruits are often blessed on this day. Many decorate their homes with marigolds (Mary's gold) to celebrate that we, too, are called to glory as she is. Psychiatrist Carl Jung saw the celebration of the Assumption as an affirmation of the power of the feminine, in Mary and in all religious consciousness and imagery.

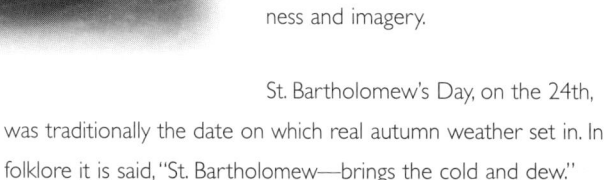

St. Bartholomew's Day, on the 24th, was traditionally the date on which real autumn weather set in. In folklore it is said, "St. Bartholomew—brings the cold and dew."

For many families, the end of August means the beginning of daily routines that have been suspended for the summer months. No more sleeping in; no more staying up late. In the quiet lull of these waning summer days, we give thanks for the memories we have gleaned, for the physical and spiritual growth of our children, for family life held dear. This is the time to "look at the birds of the air" and "consider the lilies of the field" (Matthew 6:25-33), to wonder at God's providence for all of creation, and to know that we, who are so much more valuable in God's eyes, are cared for faithfully.

CELEBRATING THE DAY

1, 12 The authors of the texts of "The Star Spangled Banner" (Francis Scott Key on the **1**st**)** and "America the Beautiful" (Katherine Lee Bates on the **12**th) both have birthdays this month. "The Star Spangled Banner" was designated as the United States national anthem in 1931. It was written as Key watched the bombardment of Fort McHenry, Maryland during the War of 1812. Bates's composition of "America the Beautiful" (1893) was inspired by the view from Pikes Peak, Colorado. Can you sing these patriotic songs?

6, 9 The United States dropped atomic bombs in 1945 on Hiroshima on the 6th and on Nagasaki on the 9th. These bombs caused a tremendous amount of destruction and loss of life. Talk about what can be done to ensure world peace so that we never have to witness another scene like that. Read *Sadako and the Thousand Paper Cranes*, by Elaine Coerr, to hear this sad story from a child's perspective. The 6th is also the Transfiguration of our Lord. On this day that we recognize the horrible powers of human destruction, we also celebrate with hope the glory of Jesus Christ, who came to save all people.

7 The picture of our planet taken from space seen for the first time on this date is a powerful one. It changed our perspective of the world and its place in the universe. People have described it as both more beautiful and more fragile than they had previously understood. What do you think of when you see it?

13, 26 Key inventors of television (the **13**th) and radio (the **26**th) have their birthdays this month. Both inventions have changed our lives dramatically. Depending on the ages in your family, talk about the kinds of programs and music you like to listen to or the impact that these inventions have had on your lives and on other families. One way to think about this is: would we spend more time with each other without these media around? Do they make our lives better...or worse?

14 Two contemporary martyrs are celebrated today, one who died in a Nazi prison camp and one who died while fighting for civil rights in the American South. A martyr is one who dies for one's faith and beliefs. Whom do you consider a martyr today?

19 Today is a good day to honor aviators and flying. Have you flown in a plane? How often? Where? People living in earlier centuries would not have believed possible what we take for granted today. Make some paper airplanes and celebrate the Wright brothers' curiosity.

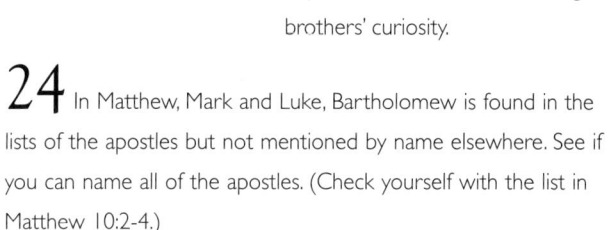

24 In Matthew, Mark and Luke, Bartholomew is found in the lists of the apostles but not mentioned by name elsewhere. See if you can name all of the apostles. (Check yourself with the list in Matthew 10:2-4.)

26 Women gained the right to vote on this date. The **8**th and the **13**th are also days to celebrate women and all they are and do. What other changes have happened for women in the last few generations? Talk about women in your own family's past and how they lived.

A U G U S T

1

✝ St. Alphonsus Liguori (1696–1787), bishop, moral theologian and founder of the Redemptorists [Catholic]
☨ Birthday of William Clark (1770–1838), American explorer and leader of the Lewis and Clark expedition
☨ Birthday of Francis Scott Key (1779–1843), American author of the text of "The Star Spangled Banner" ❀
☨ Colorado became the 38th State, 1876

2

✝ St. Eusebius of Vercelli (283?–371), early bishop and teacher
❖ Birthday of Pierre Charles L'Enfant (1754–1825), French designer of the city of Washington, D.C.

AUGUST

3

- Bourgiba's Day in Tunisia, celebrating the birthday of Habib Bourgiba, the nation's first president and leader for peace
- Independence Day in Niger in central Africa since 1960

4

- St. John Vianney (1786–1859), the Cure of Ars, priest and confessor [Catholic]
- What later became the Coast Guard was established in 1790
- Birthday of Percy Bysshe Shelley (1792–1822), English poet
- Peace Ribbon wrapped around the Pentagon, 1985

5

AUGUST

✝ Dedication of St. Mary Major, a large cathedral in Rome [Catholic]

✝ Birthday of John Eliot (1604–1690), American clergyman and "the Apostle to the Indians," translating a catechism and the Bible for them [Episcopal]

✒ Birthday of Guy de Maupassant (1850–1893), French novelist and short story writer

✒ Birthday of Conrad Aiken (1899–1973), American writer, poet and critic

@ Independence Day in Upper Volta since 1960

6

✝ Transfiguration of the Lord, when Jesus appeared in glory to the apostles (Matthew 17:1-8)

⚗ Birthday of Sir Alexander Fleming (1881–1955), Scottish bacteriologist who discovered penicillin

@ Bolivia declared independence from Peru in 1825

@ The first atomic bomb was dropped on Hiroshima, Japan, by the U.S. in 1945, killing 115,000 and injuring many times that number

AUGUST

7

✝ St. Sixtus II and Companions (died 258), martyrs in the catacombs
✝ St. Cajetan (1480–1557), priest and reformer [Catholic]
✝ John Mason Neale (1818–1866), priest, scholar and hymn writer [Episcopal]
🜚 The first pictures of Earth from space sent by Explorer VI, 1959 ✿
@ Independence Day in the Ivory Coast, remembering 1960
@ Discovery Day in Trinidad and Tobago in honor of Columbus's arrival in the Caribbean, 1498
❖ International Peace Bridge between Canada and the U.S dedicated, 1927

8

✝ St. Dominic (1170–1221), preacher and founder of the Dominican order
@ Bhutan, a Himalayan kingdom known as the "Land of Dragons," became independent in 1949
@ Tij Day, or Woman's Holiday, in Nepal ✿
❖ Birthday of Charles Bulfinch (1763–1844), first U.S. professional architect

AUGUST

9

- President Richard M. Nixon became the first U.S. President to resign from office, 1974
- The second atomic bomb was dropped on Nagasaki, Japan, 1945
- Singapore separated from Malaysia and became independent, 1965
- Smokey the Bear created, 1944

10

- St. Lawrence (died 258?), early deacon and martyr, patron saint of cooks
- Missouri became the 24th State, 1821
- Birthday of Herbert Hoover (1874–1964), 31st U.S. President
- The Smithsonian Institution was established, 1846
- Ecuador proclaimed its independence, 1830

AUGUST

11

✝ St. Clare (1194–1253), friend of St. Francis and founder of the Poor Clares
@ Independence Day in Chad since 1960
@ Coronation Day in Jordan, the anniversary of King Hussein's crowning
❖ Night of the Shooting Stars, an annual profuse meteor shower

12

☉ Airmail service began in 1918
@ Thailand Day, honoring the queen's birthday
@ Ponce de Leon arrived in Puerto Rico, 1508
❖ Birthday of Robert Mills (1781–1855), American architect and designer of the Washington Monument
❖ Birthday of Katherine Lee Bates (1859–1929), author of the text for "America the Beautiful"

13

A U G U S T

✝ Sts. Pontian and Hippolytus (died 235), priests and martyrs

✝ Jeremy Taylor (died 1667), Anglican bishop and writer [Episcopal]

💡 Birthday of John Logie Baird (1888–1946), Scottish inventor known as "the Father of Television"

@ Women's Day in Tunisia

❖ Birthday of Lucy Stone (1818–1893), American social worker and pioneer for women's rights

❖ Birthday of Annie Oakley (1860–1926), American markswoman

14

✝ St. Maximilian Mary Kolbe (1894–1941), Polish Franciscan priest who voluntarily took the place of a condemned man at Auschwitz [Catholic]

✝ Jonathan Myrick Daniels (1939–1965), seminarian killed while working for civil rights for blacks in the South [Episcopal]

@ V-J Day, or Victory Day, honoring the end of World War II, 1945

@ Bahrain proclaimed its independence in 1971

@ Pakistan established as a free nation, 1947

15

AUGUST

✝ Assumption of Mary into Heaven [Catholic and Eastern Orthodox]

✝ Feast of St. Mary the Virgin [Episcopal]

✝ Birthday of Catherine de Hueck Doherty (1896–1985), activist and founder of Madonna House in Ontario [Catholic]

✒ Birthday of Sir Walter Scott (1771–1832), Scottish author of *Ivanhoe*

@ Celebration of India's independence since 1947

@ Independence Day in the Congo since 1960

@ Korean Liberation Day, celebrating liberation from the Japanese in 1945 and the republic's inauguration in 1948

❖ Birthday of Napoleon Bonaparte (1769–1821), French emperor and general

16

✝ St. Stephen of Hungary (975–1038), king and patron of Hungary

@ Independence Day in Cyprus since 1960

@ Restoration Day in the Dominican Republic, marking the restoration of independence in 1963

17

A U G U S T

★ Birthday of Davy Crockett (1786–1836), politician and frontiersman
★ Gold was discovered in the Klondike region of Alaska, 1896
★ Birthday of Marcus Mosiah Garvey (1887–1940), black leader
@ San Martin Day in Argentina to honor the death of Jose de San Martin (1778–1850), the famous revolutionary leader
@ Independence Day in Indonesia, declared in 1945, but not fully achieved until 1949

18

✝ St. Jane Frances de Chantal (1562–1641), wife, mother, nun and founder of the Visitation order [Catholic]
✝ William Porcher DuBose (1836–1918), American priest and theologian [Episcopal]
★ Virginia Dare, first child of English parents in America, born 1587
★ Birthday of Meriwether Lewis (1774–1809), American explorer and co-leader of the Lewis and Clark expedition

AUGUST

19

✝ St. John Eudes (1601–1680), priest and preacher, who had a great devotion to the Sacred Heart and the Heart of Mary [Catholic]

✈ National Aviation Day, honoring the Wright brothers and other pioneer aviators

💡 Birthday of Orville Wright (1871–1948), American aviator and co-inventor of the airplane with his brother, Wilbur

✒ Birthday of Edith Nesbit (1858–1924), English children's author

@ Birthday of Manuel Luis Quezon (1878–1944), Philippine statesman

20

✝ St. Bernard (1091–1153), Abbot of Clairvaux, scholar and reformer

✈ Birthday of Benjamin Harrison (1833–1901), 23rd U.S. President

@ Birthday of Bernardo O'Higgins (1778–1842), Chilean general and statesman, called "the Liberator of Chile"

@ Constitution Day in Hungary since 1949

21

AUGUST

✝ St. Pius X (1835–1914), pope with poor origins who encouraged frequent reception of communion [Catholic]

⛪ Hawaii became the 50th State, 1959

♪ Birthday of William "Count" Basie (1904–1984), jazz musician

❖ The American Bar Association was organized, 1878

❖ The Lincoln-Douglas debates began in 1858, a major political event of the 19th century

22

✝ The Queenship of Mary, a traditional title given to her [Catholic]

♪ Birthday of Claude Debussy (1862–1918), French composer

@ King Richard III of England slain in battle, 1485

23

AUGUST

✝ St. Rose of Lima (1586–1617), first canonized saint of the New World [Catholic]
✒ Birthday of Edgar Lee Masters (1869–1950), American poet and author of the *Spoon River Anthology*

24

✝ St. Bartholomew, Apostle ✣
@ Independence Day for Ukraine, 1991
❖ Mount Vesuvius erupted in southern Italy, A.D. 79

25

AUGUST

✝ St. Louis, king of France (1214–1270), who ruled with justice and a concern for the poor

✝ St. Joseph Calasanz (1556–1648), scholar and founder of a community [Catholic]

♪ Birthday of Leonard Bernstein (1918–1990), American composer and conductor

@ French Liberation Day, the end of the Nazi occupation of Paris, 1944

@ Paraguay Constitution Day, since 1967

@ Uruguayan Independence Day, since 1825

26

☥ Women's Equality Day, or Susan B. Anthony Day, anniversary of approval of the 19th Amendment, giving women the right to vote, 1920 ❀

💡 Birthday of Lee De Forest (1873–1961), American inventor, known as "the Father of Radio" for his invention of the vacuum tube in 1906 ❀

💡 The first typewriter patented, 1843

@ The Sultan's Birthday, a public holiday in Zanzibar

27

AUGUST

✝ St. Monica (332?–387), mother of St. Augustine and patron saint of wives and mothers [Catholic commemoration] See May 4

✝ Mother Teresa of Calcutta (1910–), missionary to the dying [Catholic]

✝ Thomas Gallaudet (1822–1902) and Henry Winter Style (died 1890), priests and pioneers in ministry to the deaf [Episcopal]

★ Birthday of Lyndon Baines Johnson (1908–1973), 36th U.S. President

▣ Anniversary of the death of Titian (1487?–1576), Italian Renaissance painter

28

✝ St. Augustine (354–430), bishop and theologian, author of the *Confessions* and patron of students for the priesthood

✎ Birthday of Johann von Goethe (1749–1832), German poet, dramatist, philosopher, statesman and scientist

★ The Spanish landed at the site of present-day St. Augustine, Florida, 1565

★ March on Washington led by Dr. Martin Luther King, Jr., to advocate civil rights for blacks, 1963

29

✝ The Beheading of John The Baptist (Matthew 14:1-12), celebrated in the Greek Orthodox church as "the Feast of the Beheading"

AUGUST

30

@ Children's Day, a public holiday in Afghanistan honoring the children of the nation

★ Birthday of Roy Wilkins (1901–1981), American civil rights leader

31 AUGUST

✝ St. Aidan of Lindisfarne (died 651), British monk and bishop
⚱ Birthday of William Saroyan (1908–1981), American novelist and playwright
☙ Birthday of Ramon Magaysay (1907–1957), Philippine statesman
☙ Independence Day in Trinidad and Tobago since 1962
❖ Birthday of Maria Montessori (1870–1952), Italian educator and founder of the "Montessori method"

SEPTEMBER

Though the calendar year is winding down, September is a month of beginnings. School begins for many children; a new year begins in some religious traditions; the harvest begins; fall begins. The days feel a bit fresher in the mornings, and end with a cool nip in the air.

The day before the first day of school can be a special time of celebration, perhaps with opening new school supplies that have been gift wrapped and with a prayer of blessing for a school year that is healthy and full of growth. Does your family have a tradition of a picture on the morning of the first day of school before the young scholars head off? How do you mark the day?

Labor Day is the first Monday in September, although this holiday is celebrated by some other countries at other times in the year. This is a good time to talk about your "work ethic." Spend some time reflecting on the place of work in your life, and talk with your children about the value of good work.

What does work mean to you? Is it an extension of who you really are? or has it become a frustration? What is/was your favorite job? Why? What kind of workers help make our lives possible and safe—right now? How can we keep a good balance between work and family, not letting our career demands take over the time or energy that needs to be given to one another? The late Senator Paul Tsongas once remarked that no one on their deathbed ever wished that they'd spent more time at the office. How can we make sure that our priorities are clear, despite plenty of outside pressures?

Rosh Hoshanah, the Jewish New Year, also known as the Birthday of the World, is also celebrated at this time of year. This initiates the High Holy Days, and is a day when God evaluates each person's life over the past year. Jews observe the day with reflection, repentance and confession to one another, continuing these through the next ten days until Yom Kippur. A delightful custom for this day is to eat apple slices dipped in honey while saying, "May we be inscribed for a good and sweet New Year."

The Autumn Equinox usually falls around the 22nd and is called "the Day of Balance" when the hours of light and darkness are exactly equal before the darkness becomes greater until late December.

Yom Kippur, the Jewish Day of Atonement, is a day of strict fasting from sunset of the day before until after sundown on the day itself and ends the ten High Holy Days. You can read about the beginning of this tradition in Leviticus 23:26-32. On this day, the Book of Jonah is read in the synagogue to stimulate reflection on God's compassion.

This is a time to seek purification through prayer, fasting and public confession of sins, which underscores Judaism's strong belief in the social nature and effects of sin. The long day closes with the words, "The sun is low and the day is growing late. O let us come into thy gates at last." The shofar (the curved ram's horn) sounds a sustained blast that proclaims: You are forgiven.

CELEBRATING THE DAY

1, 2 Two important dates in World War II happen this month, its beginning on the **1**st with the invasion of Poland in 1939 and its ending with Japan's surrender on the **2**nd in 1945. Do you know anyone who remembers this war? If so, ask them about what it was like then. We also recognize that political unrest began in Vietnam on the last day of World War II—one war laying down its weapons and another about to pick them up. Pray for political leaders around the world who are committed to peace.

7 On this day we honor grandfathers and remember the birthday of "Grandma" Moses, an American painter. Take time today to remember your grandparents, whether alive or dead. Also in this month the **12**th is a holiday in Japan to honor the elderly, and the **27**th reminds us to appreciate those in earlier generations. What is one quality you appreciate in each of your grandparents? If any have died, tell the stories of how you remember them to be.

8 On this date we remember the birth of Mary, a little Jewish girl, a child that surely no one expected to change the world. Celebrate today all the ordinary babies around you—you never know what they will do for God. Today we also celebrate International Literacy Day. Those who cannot read are not only missing a richness in their lives, but also have a hard time functioning in society. Illiteracy always contributes to poverty. Celebrate your ability to read by starting a good book. Contact your local library to find out how to help others learn to read.

21 Read about the calling of St. Matthew in Matthew 9:9-13. Jesus got a lot of criticism for calling a "sinner" like Matthew who was a notorious tax collector known for greed and fraud. Jesus sees the heart and found a man who wanted to be closer to God. What does Jesus see when he looks at you?

26 John Chapman believed in the future. He spent his life planting apple seeds throughout the Midwest. Pray together before dinner the Johnny Appleseed song: "O the Lord's been good to me, and so I thank the Lord, for giving me the things I need, the sun and the rain and the apple seed, the Lord's been good to me. Amen."

27 Today we remember St. Vincent de Paul, whose passion for serving the poor was triggered by the last words of a dying servant. During this month (the **8**th) we celebrate the anniversary of the death of Frederic Ozanam who founded the Saint Vincent de Paul Society to honor St. Vincent. Do you have any household items or clothing that you might be able to donate to the St. Vincent de Paul Society or other agencies like the Salvation Army or Goodwill, which distribute them to others in need?

28 This is the feast of Good King Wenceslaus, about whom we sing at Christmas. Like many saints, he had a deep love for the poor. How might being a Christian make a difference in how one were a king or queen—or an elected official today?

29 Today is a feast to celebrate three key angels. Angels are messengers from God to show us how much God loves and cares for us. Do you believe in angels? Why or why not?

SEPTEMBER

1

✝ David Pendleton Oakerhater (died 1931), Cheyenne Christian convert who worked as a missionary among his people [Episcopal]

✝ Indiction, the Eastern Church's New Year

@ World War II began when German leader Adolf Hitler invaded Poland, 1939 ❀

@ Libyan Revolution Day, commemorating the assumption of power by the revolutionary council in 1969

@ Presidential Message Day in Mexico, as the Mexican Congress opens

2

✝ The Martyrs of New Guinea (1942)

remembering eight missionaries and two Christian natives betrayed and martyred [Episcopal]

★ The Treasury Department was established by Congress in 1789

@ Ho Chi Minh declared North Vietnam's independence from France, and revolts began, 1945 ❀

♪ Birthday of Lydia Liliuokalani (1838–1917), Queen of the Hawaiian Islands, overthrown but remembered for songs like "Aloha Oe"

❖ The historic London fire began, 1666, leaving four-fifths of the city in ashes

❖ Japan signed the unconditional surrender, officially ending World War II in the Pacific, 1945 ❀

SEPTEMBER

3

✝ St. Gregory the Great (540?–604), abbot, pope and reformer [Catholic commemoration] See March 12
★ The Revolutionary War ended with the Treaty of Paris, 1783
@ Independence Day in Qatar since 1971

4

✝ Paul Jones (1880–1941), American bishop and peace activist [Episcopal]
✝ Birthday of Marcus Whitman (1802–1847), American pioneer and Presbyterian missionary
★ Birthday of the city of Los Angeles, California, founded in 1781
❖ Barney Flaherty was hired as the first newsboy in the U.S., 1833

SEPTEMBER

5
- The Continental Congress met for the first time, 1774
- The first Labor Day parade held in New York City in 1882
- Be Late for Something Day in the U.S., designated by the Procrastinators Club of America

6
- Birthday of the Marquis de Lafayette (1757–1834), French military leader who served in Washington's army during the Revolution
- Somholo Day, in honor of Swaziland's independence since 1968
- Birthday of Jane Addams (1860–1935), American social worker and founder of Hull House in Chicago, a settlement house

7

SEPTEMBER

- Independence Day in Brazil, since 1822
- Birthday of Grandma (Anna Mary) Moses (1860–1961), American painter
- Grandad's Day, a day of tribute to grandfathers
- Watermelon Day, at the peak of the season

8

- The Birth of Mary, mother of Jesus
- Anniversary of the death of Frederic Ozanam (1813–1853), French founder of the St. Vincent de Paul Society to help the poor [Catholic]
- The first Catholic parish in the U.S. established at St. Augustine, Florida, 1565
- President Gerald Ford pardoned former President Nixon for any crimes during his presidency, 1974
- Birthday of Anton Dvorak (1841–1904), Czech composer famous for the *New World Symphony*
- Uganda Republic Day since 1967
- International Literacy Day, recognizing the importance of reading

SEPTEMBER

9

✝ St. Peter Claver (1581–1654), Jesuit missionary among the slaves in South America [Catholic]

✝ Sr. Constance and her companions (died 1878), nuns who helped tend those dying of yellow fever and are known with others as "The Martyrs of Memphis" [Episcopal]

★ California became the 31st State, 1850

✒ Birthday of Leo Tolstoy (1828–1910), Russian author of *War and Peace* and *Anna Karenina*

@ Bulgarian Liberation Day when the Nazis were driven out in 1944

10

✝ Alexander Crummell (1819–1898), Black American priest, missionary and leader [Episcopal]

@ Belize National Day, commemorating the 1798 Battle of St. George's Caye, when a few locals defeated the superior Spanish force

❖ Discovery Day in Hawaii, honoring Pacific and Polynesian explorers

SEPTEMBER

11

- Henry Hudson, Dutch explorer, discovered Manhattan Island, New York, 1609
- Birthday of William Sydney Porter "O. Henry" (1862–1910), American author of short stories, including "Gift of the Magi"
- Anniversary of the death of Mohammed Ali Jinnah (1876–1948), founder of a free and independent Pakistan

12

- John Henry Hobart (1775–1830), American bishop and church planter [Episcopal]
- Birthday of Alexander Campbell (1788–1866), a founder of the Disciples of Christ
- Birthday of Jesse Owens (1913–1980), American track star
- Respect for the Aged Day, a day of honor in Japan for senior citizens

SEPTEMBER

13

✟ St. John Chrysostom (died 407), bishop and preacher [Catholic commemoration] See January 27

✟ St. Cyprian [Episcopal commemoration] See September 16

❖ The Battle of Quebec, decisive in the French and Indian War, won in 1759

❖ Birthday of Walter Reed (1851–1902), army physician and surgeon, who did important research on typhoid and yellow fever

♪ Birthday of Arnold Schönberg (1874–1951), revolutionary Austrian-American composer of modern music

14

✟ The Triumph of the Cross, commemorating the finding of the cross of Jesus by St. Helena, the mother of Constantine, in 326 [Catholic]

✟ Holy Cross Day [Episcopal]

⚱ Anniversary of the death of Dante Alighieri (1265–1321), Italian poet and author of the *Divine Comedy*

@ Birthday of Jan Masaryk (1886–1948), Czechoslovak statesman

SEPTEMBER

15

- ✞ Our Lady of Sorrows, remembering Mary's suffering in love [Catholic]
- ✞ Birthday of Charles de Foucauld (1858–1916), French priest who spent his life living simply among the Tuareg people of North Africa [Catholic]
- ★ Birthday of William Howard Taft (1857–1930), 27th U.S. President
- ✒ Birthday of James Fenimore Cooper (1789–1851), American novelist famous for the *Last of the Mohicans* and others
- ☙ Central American Republics Independence Day, when Costa Rica, El Salvador, Guatemala, Honduras and Nicaragua celebrate the overthrow of Spanish rule in 1821

16

- ✞ Sts. Cornelius (died 253) and Cyprian (died 258), pope and bishop in the early church [Catholic commemoration] See September 13
- ✞ St. Ninian (died 430?), early British missionary
- ★ The Mayflower sailed from Plymouth, England, 1620
- ★ Cherokee Strip Day, commemorating the Oklahoma land rush of 1893
- ★ American Legion chartered by Congress, 1919
- ☙ Mexican Declaration of Independence Day
- ☙ Independence Day in Singapore and Malaysia since 1963

17

SEPTEMBER

† St. Robert Bellarmine (1542–1621), Jesuit scholar and bishop [Catholic]
† St. Hildegard of Bingen (1098–1179), medieval abbess, mystic, poet, composer, scientist and author
☆ Citizenship Day, honoring new Americans
❖ Birthday of Friedrich von Steuben (1730–1794), Prussian officer in the American Revolutionary War

18

† Edward Bouverie Pusey (1800–1882), priest, scholar and leader of the Oxford Movement to reform the Anglican church [Episcopal]
@ Chile Independence Day, celebrating the break with Spain in 1818
☆ George Washington laid the cornerstone of the U.S. Capitol in Washington, D.C., 1793

19

SEPTEMBER

✝ St. Januarius (died 305?), martyr and patron of blood banks and Naples
✝ Theodore of Tarsus (602–690), Archbishop of Canterbury and reformer
@ Earthquake in Mexico City in which nearly 10,000 were killed, 1985
❖ National Student Day, recognizing all students

20

✝ St. Andrew Kim Taegon (1821–1846), and
  Paul Chong Hasang and companions, a priest, seminarian and mainly lay people who were martyred in Korea, where Christianity was illegal at that time [Catholic]
✝ John Coleridge Patteson (1827–1871), bishop and companions, martyred in Melanesia [Episcopal]
☤ Farmworkers' strike began in Delano, California, 1965

SEPTEMBER

21

✝ St. Matthew, apostle, evangelist and patron of bankers, tax collectors and customs officers ✿

⚱ Anniversary of the death of Chief Joseph (1840–1904), chief of the Nez Perce tribe who led his people in an unsuccessful attempt to escape war or the reservation by fleeing to Canada

✒ Birthday of H. G. Wells (1866–1946), English novelist and historian and author of *The Invisible Man* and *The Time Machine*

@ Independence Day in Malta since 1964

22

⚗ Birthday of Michael Faraday (1791–1867), English scientist who discovered the generation of electricity by magnetism

@ Mali (formerly French Sudan) became independent of France, 1960

❖ Elephant Appreciation Day, a day to celebrate the earth's largest and most endangered land animal

SEPTEMBER

23

- Saudi Arabia Unification Day, celebrating the uniting of the political segments that now make up the nation, 1932
- The planet Neptune was first observed in 1846
- Birthday of John Lomax (1870–1948), American folklorist and founder of the American Folklore Society

24

- Birthday of F. Scott Fitzgerald (1896–1940), American novelist and author of *The Great Gatsby*
- Birthday of John Marshall (1755–1835), America lawyer and jurist, founder of the American system of constitutional law

25

SEPTEMBER

✝ St. Sergius (1314?–1392), abbot and leader of Russian Orthodoxy, patron saint of Russia

✒ Birthday of William Faulkner (1897–1962), American novelist, author of *The Sound and the Fury*, *Absalom, Absalom!* and other books

♪ Birthday of Dmitri Shostakovich (1906–1975), Russian composer

❖ Vasco de Balboa, Spanish explorer, discovered the Pacific Ocean, 1513

26

✝ Sts. Cosmas and Damian (died 303?), twin brothers, doctors and martyrs

✝ Lancelot Andrewes (died 1626), Anglican bishop, preacher, biblical scholar and author [Episcopal]

✒ Birthday of T. S. Eliot (1888–1965), British/American poet, playwright and critic

♪ Birthday of George Gershwin (1898–1937), American composer famous for *Rhapsody in Blue* and *Porgy and Bess* among others

@ Yemen Arab Republic declared, 1962

❖ Birthday of Johnny Appleseed (John Chapman) (1774–1845), who spent his life planting apple seedlings throughout the Midwestern United States 🍎

27

SEPTEMBER

✝ St. Vincent de Paul (1580?–1660), priest, missionary to the poor, reformer and founder of the Vincentians [Catholic] ❀
❖ Ancestor Appreciation Day, a day to learn about and appreciate one's forebears ❀
❖ Birthday of Thomas Nast (1840–1902), American political cartoonist who created the Democratic donkey and the Republican elephant

28

✝ St. Lawrence Ruiz (1600?–1637) and companions, brutally martyred in Japan (the first canonized Filipino martyr) [Catholic]
✝ St. Wenceslaus (907?–929), Christian king and patron of Bohemia and of the former Czechoslovakia ❀
⚓ Portuguese navigator Juan Cabrillo discovered California, 1542
@ Confucius's Birthday, or Teachers' Day, a holiday in Taiwan

29

SEPTEMBER

✝ Michael, Gabriel and Raphael, Archangels and messengers from God (Michael is the patron of policemen, grocers and radiologists; Gabriel of postmen, messengers and telephone workers; and Raphael of travelers and the blind) Also called Michaelmas

⚗ Birthday of Enrico Fermi (1901–1954), Italian physicist who pioneered work on the atomic bomb

30

✝ St. Jerome (345–420), scholar, monk and mystic, patron saint of students of scripture and librarians

🌀 Botswana became independent in 1966

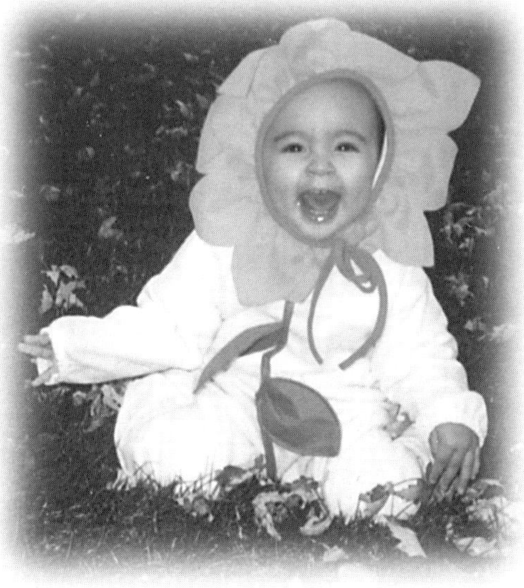

OCTOBER

The month of October brings autumn's brightly colored leaves and the end of the harvest, when we can look back to warmer times and ahead to the colder months and the sleeping of nature all around us. We enjoy a month of falling leaves and morning frost; we watch for the harvest moon at night, and ghosts and goblins on Halloween.

The Jewish Feast of Sukkot (also called Tabernacles or Booths; see Leviticus 23:39-43), which usually falls during this month, is both a harvest festival and a time to recall God's faithfulness during the 40 years that the Israelites lived in tents and wandered in the wilderness. In ancient times, the Israelites were required to journey to the Temple in Jerusalem for three major feasts: Passover, the Feast of Weeks (or Pentecost), and Sukkot.

Sukkot reminds us of the temporary nature of this life and the importance of detachment. It is an eschatological feast, that is, it looks forward to the end of time when God will gather all the world in God's *sukkot shalom*, God's "Tent of Peace."

After the seven days of Sukkot comes the Jewish Simkhat Torah, the Rejoicing in the Torah. At this time the yearly cycle of the readings from the first five books of Moses (Genesis, Exodus, Leviticus, Numbers, Deuteronomy) are completed, and the first few verses of Genesis are again read in the synagogue. Then everyone takes a turn dancing with the scrolls of the Torah in a joyful celebration.

The third Monday of the month is Hurricane Thanksgiving Day, celebrated by the people of the Virgin Islands for having been spared from the hurricanes that can ravage the area. This is a good time to pray for all those who may have experienced the destruction of a hurricane this year.

Halloween, or All Hallows' (All Saints') Eve, is a time of blending the harvest season (orange) with a focus on death and dying (black) at this time of year when winter is on its way. In pagan times, this was New Year's Eve, a night when it was feared that ghosts, goblins, witches and spirits might be abroad. Many of the customs associated with this holiday are lost in the mists of the centuries, but the need for festival and even costumes seems to be especially strong —and growing, especially among adults—at this time of year when the line seems thin between life and death.

Halloween reminds us that many of our Christian feasts and holidays have pre-Christian origins to which the Christian beliefs have added a new dimension. However, it also reminds us that the human spirit feels a deep and mysterious need for ritual and celebration that has not been quenched by modern "progress."

The Feasts of All Saints and All Souls that follow on the next two days remind Christians that the link between life and death is one of community and support, not of fear. And could there be a better symbol for the Christian life than the jack o'lantern, emptied out as we are called to be (and as Jesus was) and filled with the light? A scary prospect, it's true, but "jack" always seems to wear a smile.

CELEBRATING THE DAY

1 Today is World Vegetarian Day. Vegetarians choose not to eat meat for a variety of reasons including a respect for animals as fellow creatures. Do you know anyone who is a vegetarian? Can you go through this day without eating any meat?

2 On the feast of the guardian angels you may want to pray:
> Angel of God, my guardian dear,
> To whom God's love commits me here,
> Ever this day be at my side,
> To watch and guard, to rule and guide.

This is also the birthday of Mahatma Gandhi, an important spiritual leader and teacher of nonviolence. Older children and adults would enjoy the movie *Gandhi* about his life. Even young children can be told about nonviolence and its power to evoke change.

3, 4 The feast of St. Francis (on the **4**th) is a traditional time for blessing of pets and animals. Why not have a special prayer of blessing for any pets in your family? You might also want to read some of the stories about animals and being a country veterinarian by James Herriott on the **3**rd.

12 With older children, talk together about the culture clash that Columbus Day represents. On the one hand, the Europeans "discovered" a new and beautiful world. On the other hand, this "new world" was already occupied by many different natives. The two cultures had different histories, different agendas and different needs. How can we honor our country's past, both its European roots and its older native origins?

13 Molly Pitcher is a nickname for Mary Hays. She earned her nickname by carrying water for soldiers during the American Revolutionary War. Give each family member a nickname based on one prominent habit he or she displays. Do you like your nickname? What nickname would you rather have? What do you have to do to earn it?

15 For World Poetry Day, read some of your favorite poetry. Poets have a way of helping us think about life in a fresh way.

16 On U.N. World Food Day take some time to talk about hunger throughout the world. What would it be like not to have enough to eat today and to have to go to bed hungry? Write Bread for the World for information on what your family can do for hungry people around the world: 1100 Wayne Avenue, Suite 1000, Silver Spring, Maryland 20910

18 Saint Luke was a friend and traveling companion of the apostle Paul. Paul mentions him briefly in Colossians 4:14 and in Philemon 24. Luke is the author of the Gospel of Luke and the book of Acts. Read Luke 1:1-4 to find out why he wrote the gospel.

23 On the birthday of the inventor of the canning process, have some canned food as part of your dinner, perhaps something home-canned. What an important invention that has helped people all over the world! What could you invent that could help others live a better life?

31 Originally All Hallows' (or All Saints) Eve, this day was a time to remember saints and loved ones who had died by dressing in costumes like them and collecting food for the poor and needy. One of the ways to recall this earlier purpose might be to help collect for UNICEF, which helps children throughout the world and which we celebrate today. Also, before trick-or-treaters leave for the evening say a prayer together that they will be safe and respectful on this night of mischief.

OCTOBER

1

✝ St. Therese of Lisieux (Theresa of the Child Jesus) (1873–1897), French Carmelite nun known as the "Little Flower," patron of the missions [Catholic]

✝ St. Remigius or Remi (438–530?), bishop who helped convert the Franks

☆ Birthday of Jimmy Carter (1924–), 39th U.S. President

@ Independence Day in Nigeria since 1960

@ The People's Republic of China (Communist) established, 1949

❖ International Day for the Elderly

❖ World Vegetarian Day ❀

2

✝ Guardian Angels [Catholic] ❀

@ The Republic of Guinea declared, 1958

@ Birthday of Mohandas (Mahatma) Gandhi (1869–1948), Hindu statesman and spiritual leader of nonviolence ❀

OCTOBER

3

- Birthday of James Herriott (1916–1995), British author and veterinarian, known for *All Creatures Great and Small* and others
- Honduran holiday in honor of Francisco Morazan, a 19th-century national hero
- German reunification (East and West) in 1990

4

- St. Francis of Assisi (1181?–1226), the little poor man who lived the gospel completely and founded the Franciscan order
- Birthday of Rutherford B. Hayes (1822–1893), 19th U.S. President
- Independence Day in Lesotho since 1966
- Sputnik I, the first artificial satellite, was sent into orbit in 1957
- Birthday of Frederic Remington (1861–1909), American artist of the frontier West

OCTOBER

5

- ☆ Birthday of Chester A. Arthur (1831–1886), 21st President
- @ National Sports Day in Lesotho
- ● First radio broadcast of the World Series, 1921 (The New York Giants beat the Yankees, 5 games to 3.)
- ❖ Anniversary of the death of Tecumseh (1768–1813), Shawnee Indian chief and orator

6

- ✝ St. Bruno (1030?–1101), reformer and founder of the Carthusian monks
- ✝ St. Marie-Rose Durocher (1811–1849), founder of the Sisters of the Holy Names of Jesus and Mary [Catholic]
- ✝ William Tyndale (1495–1536), Anglican priest who translated the Bible into English [Episcopal]
- 💡 Birthday of George Westinghouse (1846–1914), American inventor of the air brake and manufacturer
- @ Universal Children's Day in Malaysia
- ❖ The American Library Association first organized, 1876

OCTOBER

7

✝ Our Lady of the Rosary, a prayer form that began in imitation of the 150 psalms and gradually took on its present form in the 16th century [Catholic]

✒ Birthday of James Whitcomb Riley (1849–1916), American poet and journalist

@ Constitution enacted in East Germany, 1949

8

🔥 The great Chicago fire began, 1871

🔥 Forest fire in Peshtigo, Wisconsin, one of the worst forest fires ever, 1871

❖ Birthday of Eddie Rickenbacker (1890–1973), American aviator and war hero

OCTOBER

9

✝ St. Denis (died 258?) and companions, bishop and martyrs
✝ St. John Leonardi (1541?–1609), reformer and religious educator [Catholic]
✝ Robert Grosseteste (died 1253), English bishop and scholar
@ Uganda declared its independence from Britain, 1962
❖ Mission Dolores (formerly Mission San Francisco de Asis), founded 1776, survivor of the 1906 earthquake and fire
❖ Lief Erikson Day, honoring the discovery of North America in the year 1000 by Norsemen

10

⚓ Naval Academy founded at Annapolis, Maryland, 1845
♪ Birthday of Giuseppi Verdi (1813–1901), Italian operatic composer
@ Double Tenth Day (10th day of 10th month), celebrated in Taiwan as the beginning of the overthrow of the Manchu dynasty, 1911
@ Sports Day in Japan, encouraging physical activity for building sound body and mind

11

OCTOBER

✝ The Second Vatican Council was opened by Pope John XXIII, 1962

★ Birthday of Eleanor Roosevelt (1884–1962), humanitarian and wife of President Franklin Roosevelt

★ Anniversary of the death of General Casimir Pulaski (1748?–1779), native of Poland and hero of the American Revolution

@ Panama Revolution Day, commemorating the 1968 revolt

❖ Birthday of Sir George Williams (1821–1905), English founder of the YMCA (Young Men's Christian Association)

12

✝ Birthday of Edith Stein (1891–1942), Jewish scholar and convert to Catholicism who became a Carmelite nun and died at Auschwitz [Catholic]

@ Columbus Day or Discovery of America Day in Spain, Central and South America, in honor of Columbus's landing in the West Indies, 1492 (observed in the U.S. on the second Monday in October) ❀

@ Independence Day in Equatorial Guinea since 1968

OCTOBER

13

✝ St. Edward (1003–1066), called "The Confessor," king and patron of England
⚓ Navy established, 1775
⚔ Birthday of "Molly Pitcher" (1754–1832), heroine of the American Revolution ❀

14

✝ St. Callistus I (died 223?), early pope and martyr
⚔ Birthday of Dwight D. Eisenhower (1890–1969), 34th U.S. President
⚔ Birthday of William Penn (1644–1718), Quaker leader and founder of Pennsylvania

15

OCTOBER

- ✞ St. Teresa of Avila (Teresa of Jesus) (1515–1582), Carmelite reformer and spiritual writer and teacher, patron saint of Spain [Catholic]
- ✞ Joseph Schereschewsky (1831–1906), Jewish-born bishop and missionary to China [Episcopal]
- ✒ World Poetry Day
- ✒ Birthday of Friedrich Nietzsche (1844–1900), German philosopher
- ✒ Birthday of Virgil (70 B.C.–19 B.C.), Roman poet, author of *The Aeneid*
- ❖ White Cane Safety Day, dedicated to the visually impaired

16

- ✞ St. Hedwig (1174?–1243), a Moravian noblewoman who helped the poor
- ✞ St. Margaret Mary Alacoque (1647–1690), who encouraged devotion to the Sacred Heart of Jesus [Catholic]
- ✞ Hugh Latimer (1490–1555) and Nicholas Ridley (died 1555), Anglican bishops and martyrs under the Catholic Queen Mary [Episcopal]
- @ United Nations World Food Day, to heighten awareness of world food issues ✿
- ✒ Birthday of Eugene O'Neill (1888–1953), American playwright
- ❖ Birthday of Noah Webster (1758–1843), creator of the American dictionary

OCTOBER

17

✝ St. Ignatius of Antioch (died 107), early bishop and martyr
✒ Black Poetry Day, in honor of black poets and Jupiter Hammon, the first black in America to publish his own verse
@ Mother's Day in Malawi
❖ LaLeche League International founded, 1956, offering support and information to breastfeeding mothers worldwide

18

✝ St. Luke the Evangelist, "the beloved physician," patron of doctors and artists ❀
★ Alaska Day, in honor of its transfer from Russia, 1867
@ Persons Day, commemorating the ruling in Canada that women were full persons legally, 1929

OCTOBER

19

✝ St. Isaac Jogues (1607–1646) and John de Brebeuf (1593–1649) and companions, Jesuits who worked among the native tribes and were martyred, the first in North America [Catholic]

✝ Henry Martyn (1781–1812), Anglican priest and missionary to India and Persia [Episcopal]

⚱ The battle of Yorktown, last major battle of the Revolutionary War, 1781

20

✝ St. Paul of the Cross (1694–1775), Italian religious, founder of the Passionist order [Catholic]

⚱ Birthday of John Dewey (1859–1952), American educator and philosopher

@ Kenyatta Day in Kenya, honoring Jomo Kenyatta (1893?–1978), the first prime minister

@ Revolution Day in Guatemala, in honor of the 1944 revolution

❖ Birthday of Sir Christopher Wren (1632–1723), English architect who designed many new buildings after the Great Fire of London

OCTOBER

21

- Birthday of Samuel Coleridge (1772–1834), English poet and essayist, author of *The Rime of the Ancient Mariner* and others
- Thomas Edison demonstrated the first incandescent light bulb that could be used for domestic purposes, 1879
- Birthday of Alfred Nobel (1833–1896), Swedish chemist who invented dynamite and other explosives, whose will established the Nobel prizes

22

- The Cuban Missile Crisis, 1962
- Birthday of Franz Liszt (1811–1886), Hungarian composer and pianist
- Jidai Matsuri, or Festival of the Eras, in Kyoto, Japan since 1895, a day to review the eras of history from the 8th to the 19th centuries

OCTOBER

23

✝ St. James of Jerusalem (died 62?), a relative of Jesus and a convert after the Resurrection, he was later bishop of Jerusalem and a martyr

✝ St. John of Capistrano (1386–1456), Franciscan preacher and reformer

💡 Birthday of Nicolas Appert (1752–1841), French chef and inventor of the canning process for preserving foods ❀

@ Hungary declared its independence, 1989

❖ The swallows of the San Juan Capistrano Mission traditionally leave for the winter, to return on March 19th

24

✝ St. Anthony Claret (1807–1870), missionary, bishop, reformer and founder of the Claretians [Catholic]

⚱ The disastrous stock market crash in 1929 that began the great depression of the 1930's

🔬 Birthday of Anton von Leeuwenhoek (1632–1723), Dutch microscopist and biologist, known as the "Father of Microscopy"

@ United Nations Day, commemorating its founding in 1945

@ Zambia Independence Day since 1964

25

O C T O B E R

★ Birthday of Richard E. Byrd (1888–1957), naval officer and polar explorer to the Antarctic
▣ Birthday of Pablo Picasso (1881–1973), Spanish-born painter and sculptor
✒ Anniversary of the death of Geoffrey Chaucer (1340?–1400), English medieval poet and author of *Canterbury Tales*
♪ Birthday of Georges Bizet (1838–1875), French composer of the opera *Carmen*

26

✝ Alfred the Great (849–899), Christian king of the West Saxons during the Viking invasions
@ South Vietnam was declared a republic, 1955, and established a constitution, 1956
❖ International Red Cross Day, established in 1863

OCTOBER

27
- Birthday of Theodore Roosevelt (1858–1919), 26th U.S. President
- Navy Day, established 1775
- Birthday of Dylan Thomas (1914–1953), Welsh poet and playwright, known especially for *A Child's Christmas in Wales*
- Cuba discovered by Columbus, 1492

28
- Sts. Simon and Jude, Apostles
- Statue of Liberty dedicated, 1886
- Birthday of Desiderius Erasmus (1467–1536), Dutch author and scholar
- Birthday of Jonas Salk (1914–1995), U.S. physician and microbiologist who developed the polio vaccine
- Hungarian Revolution, 1956
- Czechoslovakia founded as a republic, 1918 (dissolved in 1993)

29

OCTOBER

✝ James Hannington (1847–1885), Anglican bishop of Eastern Equatorial Africa, martyred with his companions near Lake Victoria [Episcopal]
@ Turkey proclaimed as a republic, 1923
❖ National Organization for Women (NOW) organized "to press for true equality for all women in America," 1966
❖ Anniversary of the death of Sir Walter Raleigh (1552–1618), English navigator, courtier, writer and colonizer

30

♔ Birthday of John Adams (1735–1826), 2nd U.S. President
⚱ Birthday of Ezra Pound (1885–1972), British/American poet and critic

OCTOBER

31

☦ Reformation Day, when Luther posted his 95 theses in Wittenberg, 1517
♜ Nevada became the 36th State, 1864
✒ Birthday of John Keats (1795–1821), English poet
❖ UNICEF Day, a day to aid the United Nations International Children's Fund ❀
❖ Halloween, All Hallows' Eve, or Beggars Night, a night for trick-or-treat in the United States ❀
❖ Birthday of Juliette Gordon Low (1860–1927), American youth leader and founder of the Girl Scouts in America
❖ National Magic Day, honoring the skills of magicians and commemorating the death of Harry Houdini in 1926

NOVEMBER

November means colder weather and warmer hearts as we remember those who have died and the saints, as we give thanks for the year's blessings, and as we begin our Advent preparations.

All Saints' Day, the 1st, can be a time to have a party where participants dress up as a favorite saint or a patron saint (the one after whom they were named). Each person may want to say something about the story of his or her saint's life. Try a rousing rendition of "When the Saints Go Marching In."

The Sunday after All Souls' Day (the 2nd) is often a Cemetery Visiting Day in Christian countries, a day to visit the graves of departed loved ones and friends, "those who have gone before us."

Thanksgiving Day in the United States is the fourth Thursday of November. What are your family's traditions on Thanksgiving? Before dinner, do you take some time to thank God for some of the year's blessings, even the ones that didn't seem like blessings?

Advent usually begins in November. The Feast of St. Andrew, first of the apostles to be called by the Lord, is celebrated on November 30th and determines the date for the season. Advent always begins on the Sunday nearest the feast of the "first called."

During Advent, the Church begins a new cycle of scripture readings. Many churches follow a three-year cycle of readings. In Year A, the gospel readings come from Matthew. In Year B, the gospel readings come from Mark. In Year C, the gospel readings come from Luke. The Gospel of John is read at different times throughout every year.

During Advent we prepare to celebrate Jesus' first coming in the flesh; we remember his promise to come again in glory; and we honor his presence among us even now. The traditional Advent wreath of greens and four candles offers a way to focus on the spiritual truths of Advent. The circle of evergreens reminds us of God's unending love and the source of our hope. The candles, usually three purple and one pink, are lighted on each Sunday before Christmas (the pink is for the third Sunday of Advent), one on the first Sunday, two on the second, and so on. Week by week we experience more light and less darkness. "O Come, O Come, Emmanuel" can be sung as the candles are lit.

The nativity scene—minus the Christ child who doesn't appear until Christmas Eve—should be the center focus for the season, not the Christmas tree. Some families place the nativity figures around the room at various distances from the nativity scene, and each day the figures "travel" a little closer to it, including the three wise ones, who have the farthest to come.

A good way to encourage the spirit of giving during Advent is to have Krist kindls (German for "Christ child"). Each family member draws the name of another in the family for whom he or she can be a secret Advent friend. These Advent friends are like the hidden Christ child, gracing each other's lives with kind deeds done anonymously, with special prayers, or with homemade gifts. On Christmas, each family member can guess who was his or her Krist kindl.

Advent calendars, with a window to open for each day of December until Christmas Eve, can help us mark the days to this season of giving.

CELEBRATING THE DAY

1 Are there some people you know who seem to be "saints," that is, they love God and others deeply? Talk about it as a family.

2 This is a day to pray in a special way for all those we know who have died. Why not make a list together and remember what a gift those people were in your lives?

6 On the birthday of John Philip Sousa, play one of his marches and march around the room.

11 Do you know someone who is a veteran, who served in a war? Ask them about their experiences. What do you think our nation would be like today if it had not fought any of its wars? Today is also the feast of St. Martin of Tours, who refused to continue to fight in the Roman army as a Christian. What do you think: When should Christians fight and when should they help make peace by refusing to fight?

13, 29, 30 There are several excellent authors born this month, including Robert Louis Stevenson (on the **13**th) whose *A Child's Garden of Verses* and *Treasure Island* are excellent for different age groups. There's also Louisa Mae Alcott (*Little Women* and *Little Men*) and Madeleine L'Engle (*A Wrinkle in Time* and others) and C.S. Lewis (*The Chronicles of Narnia*), all on the **29**th, and Mark Twain (*Tom Sawyer* and *Huckleberry Finn* and others) on the **30**th. Take your pick and enjoy!

17 Celebrate the smell and touch of warm homemade bread. If you're not a breadmaker and you don't have an automatic one, don't worry. Just buy some frozen dough from the market—thaw, bake and enjoy.

18 Today is the "birthday" of Mickey Mouse. Who is your favorite cartoon character and why?

21 On World Hello Day, see if you can say it in five different languages, such as French (Bonjours), Spanish (Hola), German (Guten Tag) or Japanese (Konichiwa.) You already know at least one language!

22 Ask someone who remembers the assassination of President John Kennedy what they were doing when they heard the news of his death.

30 St. Andrew was the first disciple whom Jesus called. Read about his meeting with Jesus in John 1:35-42. What was the first thing Andrew did after he met Jesus?

NOVEMBER

1

✝ All Saints, a day for the everyday saints, not just those well known ❀

◊ Birthday of Stephen Crane (1871–1900), American author of *The Red Badge of Courage*

◊ Author's Day, celebrated since 1928 to honor the work of writers and encourage more quality writing

@ Algerian Revolution Day, commemorating the revolution by the National Liberation Front against the French, 1954

@ Memorial Day in the Republic of Togo

2

✝ All Souls, a day to pray for all who have died
   (In Mexico this is Dia de Muertes, Day of the Dead; in Portugal it is Dia de Finados) ❀

★ Birthday of Warren G. Harding (1865–1923), 29th U.S. President

★ Birthday of James Polk (1795–1849), 11th U.S. President

★ North Dakota became the 39th State, 1889

★ South Dakota became the 40th State, 1889

@ Birthday of Daniel Boone (1734–1820), American pioneer, explorer, surveyor

NOVEMBER

3

✝ St. Martin de Porres (1579–1639), of mixed race, he cared for the poor and sick in Lima, Peru as a Dominican, patron of interracial justice [Catholic]

✝ Richard Hooker (1553–1600), Anglican theologian [Episcopal]

★ Birthday of Stephen Austin (1793–1836), "the Father of Texas"

@ Panama declared its independence from Colombia, 1903

@ Culture Day in Japan, to encourage interest in freedom and cultural activities, formerly the Emperor Meiji's birthday

✒ Birthday of William Cullen Bryant (1794–1878), American poet

4

✝ St. Charles Borromeo (1538–1584), reformer and bishop and patron of religious instruction and libraries [Catholic]

@ UNESCO (United Nations Educational, Scientific and Cultural Organization) established, 1946

❖ Birthday of Will Rogers (1879–1935), American humorist and author

NOVEMBER

5

@ Guy Fawkes Day in Canada and Great Britain, remembering the "Gunpowder Plot" to blow up Parliament and the king in 1605

6

♪● Birthday of James Naismith (1861–1939), Canadian-American inventor of basketball as a class assignment in 1891
♪ Birthday of John Philip Sousa (1854–1932), American bandmaster and composer of marches
@ Gustavus Adolphus Day, honoring the Swedish king who died in battle in 1632
♪ Birthday of Ignace Jan Paderewski (1860–1941), Polish pianist, composer and statesman

7

NOVEMBER

✝ Willibrord (658?–739), Archbishop of Utrecht and missionary among the Germanic peoples
@ The Bolshevik Revolution occurred in Russia, 1917
✒ Birthday of Albert Camus (1913–1960), French author of *The Stranger*, *The Plague* and other works
⚗ Birthday of Marie Curie (1867–1934), Polish-French chemist and physicist, co-discoverer with her husband of radium, first woman to win the Nobel Prize and first person to win two Nobel Prizes (for physics, 1903; for chemistry, 1911)

8

✝ Birthday of Dorothy Day (1897–1980), founder of the Catholic Worker and devoted to serving the poor and to nonviolence [Catholic]
✝ Anniversary of the death of John Duns Scotus (1265?–1308), Scottish scholastic theologian
★ Montana became the 41st State, 1889
☄ Birthday of Edmund Halley (1656–1742), English astronomer and student of comets
✒ Birthday of Margaret Mitchell (1900–1949), American author of *Gone with the Wind*

NOVEMBER

9

✝ Dedication of St. John Lateran, the cathedral of the diocese of Rome [Catholic]

✡ Crystal Night, the anniversary of the street riots when Nazi storm troopers raided Jewish homes and synagogues in Berlin in 1938, named because of the shattered glass that night

10

✝ St. Leo the Great (died 461), early pope and preacher

✝ Birthday of Martin Luther (1483–1546), German religious reformer, translator of the Bible and writer of hymns

⚔ Marine Corps founded, 1775

✒ Birthday of Oliver Goldsmith (1730–1774), Irish author and poet

✒ Birthday of Vachel Lindsay (1879–1931), American poet

❦ Hero Day and Youth Day in Indonesia

NOVEMBER

11

✟ St. Martin of Tours (316?–397), a conscientious objector, monk and bishop, patron of soldiers, horsemen, tailors, beggars and reformed drunkards ❀

★ Veterans' Day, formerly called Armistice Day, honors member of the Armed Forces that served in war ❀

♠ Birthday of Fyodor Dostoyevsky (1821–1881), Russian novelist famous for *The Brothers Karamazov* and *Crime and Punishment*

★ Washington became the 42nd State, 1889

12

✟ St. Josaphat (1580?–1623), a bishop of Lithuania who worked for a reunion of Eastern Christians with Rome [Catholic]

✟ Charles Simeon (died 1836), Anglican preacher and reformer [Episcopal]

★ Birthday of Elizabeth Cady Stanton (1815–1902), American woman-suffrage reformer

♠ Birthday of Juana Ines de La Cruz (1651–1695), Mexican poet-nun

@ Austria declared itself a republic, 1918

NOVEMBER

13

✝ St. Francis Xavier Cabrini (1850–1917), who worked among the American immigrant poor, starting hospitals and orphanages [Catholic]

⚱ Birthday of Robert Louis Stevenson (1850–1894), Scottish novelist and poet, famous for *Treasure Island* and *A Child's Garden of Verses*

@ The King's Birthday, a holiday in Laos

14

✝ Consecration of Samuel Seabury (1729–1784), first American Episcopal bishop [Episcopal]

💡 Birthday of Robert Fulton (1765–1815), American civil engineer and inventor of the steamboat

🖼 Birthday of Claude Monet (1840–1926), French landscape painter

@ Birthday of Jawaharlal Nehru (1889–1964), first prime minister of India

♪ Birthday of Aaron Copland (1900–1990), American composer of *Appalachian Spring* and *Fanfare for the Common Man*, among others

⚱ Birthday of Astrid Lindgren (1907–   ), Swedish author of the Pippi Longstocking stories

NOVEMBER

15

✝ St. Albert the Great (1206–1280), Dominican scholar and patron of scientists and philosophers
☄ Birthday of Sir William Herschel (1738–1822), Anglo-German astronomer who built his own telescope and discovered the planet Uranus
✒ Birthday of Marianne Moore (1887–1972), American poet
☺ 7-5-3 Festival Day in Japan, when parents give thanks for children, especially girls ages 3 and 7 and boys ages 3 and 5
🖼 Birthday of Georgia O'Keeffe (1887–1986), American painter

16

✝ St. Margaret of Scotland (1050?–1093), queen, mother and friend to the poor
✝ St. Gertrude (1256?–1302), mystic and patron of the West Indies
✝ Six Jesuits and two women were martyred at the Central American University in El Salvador, 1989
★ Oklahoma became the 46th State, 1907
♪ Birthday of W.C. Handy (1873–1958), American composer and "Father of the Blues"

17

NOVEMBER

✝ St. Elizabeth of Hungary (1207–1231), mother, widow, friend to the poor and patron of Catholic charities and of the Franciscan Third Order [Catholic commemoration] See November 19
✝ St. Hugh of Lincoln, Carthusian monk and bishop
@ The Suez Canal in Egypt opened in 1869
❖ Homemade Bread Day, a day to remember and enjoy the making, baking and eating of homemade bread 🌸

18

✝ St. Rose Philippine Duchesne (1769–1852), French religious missionary in the early American Midwest [Catholic]
✝ Dedication of the Churches of Peter and Paul, two churches in Rome [Catholic]
✝ St. Hilda (614–680), abbess of Whitby and advisor to kings and others
💡 Birthday of Louis Daguerre (1789–1851), French inventor of an early kind of photography, the daguerreotype process
♪ Birthday of Sir William Gilbert (1836–1911), British composer with Arthur Sullivan of popular operettas
❖ Birthday of Jacques Maritain (1882–1973), French philosopher and scholar
❖ Birthday of Nils Nordenskjold (1832–1901), Swedish Arctic explorer
❖ "Birthday" of Mickey Mouse (1928), Walt Disney's cartoon creation appeared in *Steamboat Willie* 🌸

NOVEMBER

19

- ✝ St. Elizabeth of Hungary [Episcopal commemoration] See November 17
- ★ Gettysburg Address given by President Abraham Lincoln, 1863
- ★ Birthday of James Garfield (1831–1881), 20th U.S. President
- ★ Puerto Rico discovered by Chrisopher Columbus, 1493
- @ Official birthday of the Prince of Monaco

20

- ✒ Birthday of Selma Lagerlof (1858–1940), Swedish novelist, author of children's stories collected as *The Wonderful Adventures of Nils*
- @ Mexico Revolution Day, anniversary of the revolt against the dictatorship of Porifirio Diaz in 1910
- @ The Declaration of the Rights of the Child adopted by the United Nations, 1959
- @ The Nuremburg war trials began after World War II, 1945

NOVEMBER

21
✝ Presentation of Mary, dedicated to God at a young age [Catholic]
☆ North Carolina became the 12th State, 1789
✒ Birthday of Jean Voltaire (1694–1778), French author and freethinker, known for *Candide*
@ World Hello Day

22
✝ St. Cecilia (c. 4th century), Roman martyr and patron saint of musicians, religious music and of organ builders
☆ President John F. Kennedy assassinated in Dallas, Texas, 1963
✒ Birthday of George Eliot (1819–1880), English novelist, known for *Silas Marner* and *Mill on the Floss*
@ Birthday of Charles de Gaulle (1890–1970), French statesman and president

23

NOVEMBER

- ✝ St. Clement I (died 101?), an early pope and patron of stonecutters
- ✝ St. Columban (543?–615), Irish missionary to Europe and abbot
- ★ Birthday of Franklin Pierce (1804–1869), 14th U.S. President
- @ Labor-Thanksgiving Day in Japan, a day to give thanks and to rest
- @ First recorded strike, Egypt in 1170 B.C.
- 🖼 Birthday of Jose Clement Orozco (1883–1949), Mexican painter

24

- ✝ St. Andrew Dung-Lac and companions, 117 martyrs who met death between 1820 and 1862 in different persecutions in Vietnam [Catholic]
- ✝ Anniversary of the death of John Knox (1505?–1572), Scottish preacher and leader of the Protestant Reformation in Scotland
- ✝ Birthday of Friar Junipero Serra (1713–1784), Spanish Franciscan priest-missionary and founder of the California missions [Catholic]
- ♪ Birthday of Scott Joplin (1868–1917), American ragtime composer
- ★ Birthday of Zachary Taylor (1784–1850), 12th U.S. President
- @ Anniversary of the New Regime in Zaire, marking the end of rebellion and the start of a new government, 1964

25

NOVEMBER

✝ St. Catherine of Alexandria, a popular saint whose origins are lost in legend, patron of philosopher, jurists and women students
✝ Birthday of Pope John XXIII, born Angelo Roncalli (1881–1963), who called the Second Vatican Council and worked for church unity
❖ Birthday of Andrew Carnegie (1835–1919), American industrialist and philanthropist
❖ Birthday of Carrie Nation (1846–1911), American temperance leader who used a hatchet in her campaign against saloons

26

☥ Anniversary of the death of Sojourner Truth (1797–1883), American abolitionist and lecturer on equal rights
@ Independence Day in Lebanon, commemorating the end of French rule in 1941

27

NOVEMBER

- Birthday of Jose Asuncion Silva (1865–1896), Colombian poet
- Birthday of Chaim Weizmann (1874–1952), Israeli statesman and first president of Israel

28

- Kamehameha IV (1835–1864) and
  Emma (died 1885), king and queen of Hawaii who asked for missionaries to be sent [Episcopal]
- Birthday of Henry Bacon (1866–1924), American architect of the Lincoln Memorial in Washington, D.C.
- Birthday of Norman Rockwell (1894–1978), American illustrator and painter
- Independence Day in several countries: Albania (since 1912), Burundi (since 1966), Chad (since 1958) and Mauritania (since 1960)
- Accession of the Ruler of Abu Dhabi, a holiday in the United Arab Emirates

29

NOVEMBER

✝ National Council of the Churches of Christ established, 1950

⌁ Birthday of Louisa May Alcott (1832–1888), American novelist, author of *Little Women* and others ✿

⌁ Birthday of Madeleine L'Engle (1918–), American author of *A Wrinkle in Time* and others ✿

⌁ Birthday of C. S. Lewis (1898–1963), English novelist and author of *The Chronicles of Narnia* and others ✿

@ President Tubman's Birthday in Liberia, honoring its first president, William Tubman (1895–1971)

30

✝ St. Andrew, apostle and patron of Scotland, fishermen and golfers ✿

⌁ Birthday of Jonathan Swift (1667–1745), English poet and satirist, remembered especially for *Gulliver's Travels*

⌁ Birthday of Samuel Langhorne Clemens "Mark Twain" (1835–1910), American humorist and author of *Tom Sawyer* and others ✿

@ Birthday of Sir Winston Churchill (1874–1965), British statesman

@ Barbados Independence Day, since 1966

@ Yemen Independence Day, since 1967

DECEMBER

December is a month of contradictions. We feel the cold of winter, and the warmth of family gatherings. The long darkness of night surrounds us, but the many-colored lights of the season shine around us. The life of nature seems to die, but we focus on the birth of a Child.

The 1st begins Rohatsu, an annual eight-day "retreat" observed by many Buddhists throughout the world, culminating in the celebration of the Enlightenment of the Buddha on December 8th.

Another festival of light enters this month with the Jewish Hannukah during which an additional candle is lighted each evening for eight days on a candelabra known as a menorah. The feast celebrates the rededication of the Temple by a group of Jewish rebels known as the Maccabees. The dreidel, a traditional game for the holiday, is played with a spinning top, which reminds us of the earth spinning on its axis.

On the 16th, the Posadas begin. "Posadas" means lodgings in Spanish, and in Mexico, children dress as Mary and Joseph and go from house to house seeking shelter. The processions continue for seven days, and the last house each evening is the site of prayers and feasting.

Around the 21st we watch for the Winter Solstice, the shortest day and the longest night of the year. From this day on, the days will each get longer until mid-summer.

The Sunday before Christmas is the Sunday of the Genealogy in the Eastern Churches. On this day, all the ancestors of Christ, "the holy ones who pleased God, from Adam and Eve to the betrothed of the Mother of God," are remembered.

The 26th begins the observance of Kwanzaa, a cultural festival of black Americans begun in the 60's and celebrated for a week until January 1st. Candles of red, green and black are placed in a holder called a kinara. One candle is lighted each day for a principle that African Americans should live by, including Umoja (unity), Kujichagulia (self-determination), Ujima (collective work and responsibility), Ujamaa (cooperative economics), Nia (purpose), Kuumba (creativity) and Imani (faith). Kwanzaa is a good example of the basic human need for ritual celebration and the "self-generation" of such rituals where they are lacking.

The Sunday between Christmas and New Year's (or December 30 if there is no Sunday between the two) is the Feast of the Holy Family. This is an excellent opportunity to reflect on how your family and other families of various sizes and shapes are all holy in many very ordinary and daily ways. We may not feel or even look holy, but as we go about loving and serving one another, we *are* a holy family.

C E L E B R A T I N G   T H E   D A Y

6 St. Nicholas is the source of our tradition of Santa Claus. Children in Holland put their shoes out on the eve of his feast and find treats in them the next morning, unless they've been bad, when they find a lump of coal. Celebrating St. Nicholas's feast can help to remind us all of who Santa Claus really was. It also takes a little pressure off the long wait until Christmas Eve.

9, 30 Besides books and stories for the Christmas season, don't forget the *Uncle Remus* stories of Joel Chandler Harris and the Babar books of de Brunhoff (both born on the **9**th), and *The Jungle Book* and other delightful stories of Rudyard Kipling (born on the **30**th).

12 Our Lady of Guadalupe is an important feast to the Hispanic peoples of the world. How about some Mexican food tonight to celebrate?

16 The Boston Tea Party in 1773 accelerated the separation of the colonies from British rule. Remember this turning point in American history by having a cup of tea.

17 The O Antiphons are a series of seven prayers of longing for the coming, or advent, of Jesus as the Messiah or Emmanuel, which means "God with us." They have a long tradition in the Christian community and are a way of preparing for the feast of Christmas.

22 Visit your local library and ask for a list of Newbury Medal winners. Choose a couple to read and find out why they won.

24 On Christmas Eve, try to make sure that the nativity scene is the focus of attention, not the Christmas tree and its presents. One way to do this is to now place the infant Jesus in the scene— missing until he was "born"— perhaps singing a song like "Silent Night," composed on this date.

25 The twelve days of Christmas begin with Christmas day and go until the Feast of the Epiphany. Make the entire time a season of celebration.

27 St. John has been thought by many to have been the "beloved disciple" referred to in the Gospel of John. We do know that he and his brother, James, along with the apostle Peter were the three disciples who were closest to Jesus during his earthly ministry. They were granted the vision of his transfiguration and they were invited to accompany him during his night of prayer before the passion. In what ways has Jesus shown you that you are beloved?

31 On New Year's Eve why not have a blessing of clocks and watches and (new) calendars in gratitude for the gift of time and for the richness that the past year has brought? What are your favorite memories of the past year? What are your hopes for the coming year? Some families make a "time capsule" to be opened the following year on New Year's Eve so that they can recall what was happening a year before.

DECEMBER

1

† Nicholas Ferrar (1592–1637), deacon and founder of Little Gidding, an Anglican religious community [Episcopal]

☫ Rosa Parks kept her seat on a Montgomery bus instead of giving it to a white passenger, helping begin the civil rights movement, 1955

@ Iceland declared its independence from Denmark, 1918

@ Matilda Newport Day, in Liberia to honor a pioneer widow who ignited a cannon with her pipe during a siege in 1822 and saved her country

@ Central African Republic declared its independence, 1958

❖ Rohatsu, a Buddhist retreat, begins

2

† Four women missionaries (Jean Donovan, Sisters Maura Clarke, Ita Ford and Dorothy Kazel) were martyred in El Salvador, 1980 [Catholic]

† Channing Moore Williams (1829–1910), American missionary bishop in China and Japan [Episcopal]

@ Pan American Health Day, a day to focus on hemispheric cooperation in the field of public health

December

3

- ✝ St. Francis Xavier (1506–1552), Jesuit missionary to the Far East [Catholic]
- Illinois became the 21st State, 1818
- Birthday of Joseph Conrad (1857–1924), Polish-born English novelist, author of *Heart of Darkness*, *Lord Jim* and others
- Birthday of Cleveland Abbe (1838–1916), American meteorologist known as "the Father of the Weather Bureau"
- ❖ The first human heart transplanted by Dr. Christian Barnard in Cape Town, South Africa, 1967
- ❖ Sir Rowland Hill Day, in honor of the man who introduced the first postage stamps in the world in England in 1840

4

- ✝ St. John Damascene (676?–749), scholar, reformer and theologian
- Birthday of Thomas Carlyle (1795–1881), Scottish essayist and historian
- Day of the Artisans, a day in Mexico to honor the workers of the nation

DECEMBER

5

✞ Clement of Alexandria (c. 210), priest, apologist and philosopher
✞ St. Nicholas' Eve is celebrated in European countries with stories of the life and works of St. Nicholas, 3rd-century bishop of Myra
♚ Birthday of Martin Van Buren (1782–1862), 8th President
❖ Birthday of Walt Disney (1901–1966), American film producer and pioneer in animated cartoons
@ Discovery Day in Haiti, commemorating its discovery by Christopher Columbus in 1492

6

✞ St. Nicholas (died 350?), bishop of Myra and patron of Russia, sailors, and children, traditionally brings treats on his feast day to children in Europe ❀
✒ Birthday of Joyce Kilmer (1886–1918), American poet remembered for *Trees*
@ Finland declared its independence from Russia in 1917
@ Quito, Ecuador, was founded by the Spanish in 1534

DECEMBER

7

- St. Ambrose (340?–397), bishop, scholar and preacher
- Japanese planes attacked Pearl Harbor, the Philippines and Guam, 1941
- Birthday of Willa Cather (1873–1947), American author of *O Pioneers!*, *My Antonia* and other works
- Delaware became the 1st State, 1787
- Birthday of Giovanni Bernini (1598–1680), Italian architect who helped work on St. Peter's in Rome

8

- Feast of the Immaculate Conception of Mary, "full of grace" [Catholic]
- Birthday of Jean Sibelius (1865–1957), Finnish composer famous for *Finlandia*
- Birthday of Padraic Colum (1881–1972), Irish poet, folklorist and dramatist
- Birthday of Eli Whitney (1765–1825), American inventor of the cotton gin
- Beach Day, or Blessing of the Waters Day, in Uruguay before beach season
- Mother's Day in Spain, long associated with the Feast of the Immaculate Conception
- Buddha's Enlightenment

DECEMBER

9

- Blessed Juan Diego (16th century), the Mexican Indian to whom Our Lady of Guadalupe appeared (See December 12) [Catholic]
- Birthday of John Milton (1608–1674), English poet best known for *Paradise Lost*
- Birthday of Joel Chandler Harris (1848–1908), American author and journalist know for his *Uncle Remus* stories
- Birthday of Jean de Brunhoff (1899–1937), author of children's stories about Babar the Elephant King
- Independence Day in Tanzania since 1961
- The John Birch Society was founded, 1958

10

- United Nations Human Rights Day, honoring the Declaration signed in 1948
- Mississippi became the 20th State, 1817
- Birthday of Emily Dickinson (1830–1886), American poet
- Birthday of Thomas Hopkins Gallaudet (1787–1851), American pioneer teacher of the deaf
- The Nobel Prizes are awarded on this day, the anniversary of the death of the founder, Alfred Bernhard Nobel (See October 21)

DECEMBER

11

- St. Damasus I (305?–384), early pope
- Indiana became the 19th State, 1816
- Birthday of Robert Koch (1843–1910), German bacteriologist who discovered the bacili of tuberculosis and cholera
- Scaling Day in Geneva, Switzerland, honoring the night in 1602 when the city was saved from the Savoyards (Chocolate bonbons are sold to recall the soup pots from which hot water was thrown on the invaders scaling the city walls.)
- Upper Volta became a republic in 1958

12

- Our Lady of Guadalupe, who appeared to Juan Diego, a poor Mexican Indian, in 1531, an important devotion for Hispanic Catholics [Catholic]
- Pennsylvania became the 2nd State, 1787
- Washington, D.C., established as the permanent capital, 1800
- Kenya declared independent in 1963
- The United Nations Committee on the Peaceful Uses of Outer Space established, 1959
- The first transatlantic radio signal sent by Italian Guglielmo Marconi, 1901

13

DECEMBER

✝ St. Lucy (died 304), martyr and patron of writers, of those with eye trouble and of lights (In Sweden young girls wear crowns of lights and serve special saffron buns to their families.)

@ New Zealand discovered by Dutch explorer Abel Tasmand, 1642

14

✝ St. John of the Cross (1541–1591), Carmelite priest, mystic and poet [Catholic]

★ Alabama became the 22nd State, 1819

DECEMBER

15

- Bill of Rights Day, in honor of the ratification of the first ten amendments to the Constitution
- Autonomy granted to the Netherland Antilles in 1954
- Anniversary of the death of Sitting Bull (1834?–1890), famous medicine man and leader of the Hunkpapa Sioux
- Zamenhof Day, in honor of Dr. Ludwik Zamenhof, the founder of Esperanto, the international language

16

- First day of Posadas, an Hispanic tradition of nine days of procession with Mary and Joseph, who are looking for a place to stay in Bethlehem
- The Boston Tea Party, when the colonists boarded a British ship and dumped tea into the harbor rather than pay the British tax, 1773
- Birthday of Jane Austen (1775–1817), English novelist, remembered for *Pride and Prejudice* and others
- Birthday of Ludwig van Beethoven (1770–1827), German composer
- Birthday of Noel Coward (1899–1973), British playwright
- Birthday of Margaret Mead (1901–1978), American anthropologist

17 DECEMBER

✞ O Antiphons begin: *O Wisdom, O Holy Word of God, you govern all creation with your strong yet tender care. Come and show your people the way to salvation.*

 Colombia declared its independence from Spain, 1819

 Birthday of John Greenleaf Whittier (1807–1892), American poet, abolitionist and journalist

❖ Wright Brothers Day, to honor their first flight near Kitty Hawk, North Carolina, 1903

18

✞ *O sacred Lord of ancient Israel, who showed yourself to Moses in the burning bush, who gave him the holy law on Sinai mountain: come, stretch out your might hand to set us free.*

 New Jersey became the 3rd State, 1787

✞ Birthday of Charles Wesley (1707–1788), Anglican preacher and hymn writer [Episcopal]

 Birthday of Stethen Biko (1946–1977), leader of South African blacks who died while in jail

DECEMBER

19

✝ *O Flower of Jesse's stem, you have been raised up as a sign for all peoples; kings stand silent in your presence; the nations bow down in worship before you. Come, let nothing keep you from coming to our aid.*

❖ Benjamin Franklin's *Poor Richard's Almanack* first published, 1732

20

✝ *O Key of David, O royal Power of Israel controlling at your will the gate of heaven: come, break down the prison walls of death for those who dwell in darkness and the shadow of death; and lead your captive people into freedom.*

🏛 Louisiana Territory transferred from France to the U.S., 1803

21

DECEMBER

✝ *O Radiant Dawn, splendor of eternal light, sun of justice: come, shine on those who dwell in darkness and the shadow of death.*

✝ St. Peter Canisius (1521–1597), Jesuit scholar, teacher and preacher [Catholic]

✝ St. Thomas the Apostle [Episcopal commemoration] See July 3

⚱ Pilgrims landed in Plymouth, Massachusetts, 1620

@ Nepal became independent in 1923

22

✝ *O King of all the nations, the only joy of every human heart; O Keystone of the mighty arch of humankind, come and save the creature you fashioned from the dust.*

✒ Anniversary of the death of John Newbery (1767), English publisher and bookseller specializing in children's books, in whose honor the Newbery Medal is given yearly for the outstanding children's book ✿

♪ Birthday of Giacomo Puccini (1858–1924), Italian operatic composer best known for *Madame Butterfly*

❖ International Arbor Day, to encourage worldwide interest in trees

DECEMBER

23

✝ *O Emmanuel, king and lawgiver, desire of the nations, Savior of all people, come and set us free, Lord our God.*

✝ St. John of Kanty (1390?–1473), Polish priest, teacher and lover of the poor

💡 First transistor invented by Americans John Bardeen, William Brattain and William Shockley in 1947

❖ Birthday of Joseph Smith (1805–1844), founder of the Church of Jesus Christ of Latter Day Saints (Mormons)

24

✝ Christmas Eve ❀

♪ The carol "Silent Night" written by an Austrian priest, Fr. Joseph Mohr, and his organist, Franz Gruber, in 1818 ❀

@ Laos declared its independence, 1953

@ Libya achieved independence, 1951

25

DECEMBER

✞ Christmas Day, the Feast of the Nativity of Jesus Christ ✤
@ Taiwan (Republic of China) adopted a constitution, 1946
❖ Birthday of Clara Barton (1821–1912), American philanthropist and organizer of the Red Cross

26

✞ Second Day of Christmas
✞ St. Stephen (died 36?), the first martyr (Acts 7) and patron of Hungary, of horses and of stonecutters
@ Boxing Day in Great Britain
❖ First day of Kwanzaa, an African-American festival of seven days, focusing on seven principles of black culture

DECEMBER

27

✝ Third Day of Christmas
✝ St. John, apostle and evangelist ❀
⚗ Birthday of Louis Pasteur (1822–1895), French chemist and founder of microbiological sciences and preventive medicine

28

✝ Fourth Day of Christmas
✝ Holy Innocents, remembering the boys two years and under killed by Herod in search of Jesus, the newborn King (Matthew 2)
♔ Birthday of Woodrow Wilson (1856–1924), 28th U.S. President
♔ Iowa became the 29th State, 1846
@ King Birenda's Day, a holiday in Nepal
❖ Chewing gum patented by American William Semple in 1869

29

D E C E M B E R

✝ Fifth Day of Christmas

✝ Thomas Becket (1118–1170), Archbishop of Canterbury and martyr

★ Birthday of Andrew Johnson (1808–1875), 17th U.S. President

★ Texas became the 28th State, 1845

★ Over 200 Sioux slaughtered at Wounded Knee, South Dakota, by the U.S. Cavalry, 1890

♪ Birthday of Pablo Casals (1876–1973), Spanish-born cellist

30

✝ Sixth Day of Christmas

✎ Birthday of Rudyard Kipling (1865–1936), English novelist, poet and short story writer, famous for *Jungle Book* ❀

❖ Birthday of Simon Guggenheim (1867–1941), American capitalist and philanthropist

31 DECEMBER

✝ Seventh Day of Christmas

✝ St. Sylvester I (died 335), who was pope as the church became legal during the reign of the Emperor Constantine

⛴ Ellis Island in New York harbor opened to receive all immigrants to the country, 1890

@ Omisoka Day in Japan, a day for taking stock and the payment of debts

❖ New Year's Eve, a time to celebrate and watch the old year out and the new year in ❀

BIBLIOGRAPHY

Resources for Family Prayer and Ritual

Bishops' Committee on the Liturgy. National Conference of Catholic Bishops. *Catholic Household Blessings and Prayers*. U.S. Catholic Conference, 1988. A rather formal resource for a wide variety of occasions.

DeGidio, Sandra. *Enriching Faith Through Family Celebrations*. Twenty-Third Publications, 1989. A good source book on ritual in general and specific rituals throughout the liturgical year. Some prayers may be too long for very young children.

Finley, Kathleen. *Dear God: Prayers for Families with Children*. Twenty-Third Publications, 1995. A broad assortment of prayers for seasons of the year as well as times of the day, accompanied by delightful illustrations. Especially helpful for families with preschoolers and grade-school children.

Finley, Mitch. *Your Family in Focus: Appreciating What You Have, Making It Even Better*. Ave Maria Press, 1993. A good introduction to seeing daily family life as holy.

Hays, Edward. *Prayers for the Domestic Church: A Handbook for Worship in the Home*. Forest of Peace Books, 1979. An excellent source for prayers, but best for families with adolescents or adults due to the length of the prayers.

Herbert, Christopher. *Prayers for Children*. Forward Movement Publications, 1993. Prayers for many occasions and seasons, especially for families with grade school children.

National Conference of Catholic Bishops. *Follow The Way of Love: A Pastoral Message of the U.S. Catholic Bishops to Families*. United States Catholic Conference, 1994. This is an excellent document that clearly affirms the holiness of families as the domestic church.

Nelson, Gertrud Mueller. *To Dance With God: Family Ritual and Community Celebration*. Paulist Press, 1986. A prayerful meditation on the seasons of the Church year with many ideas for family ritual, drawn primarily from a rich European heritage.

Roberto, John, et al. *Family Rituals and Celebrations*. (Catholic Families Series) Don Bosco, 1992. A good resource for family prayer, mainly for families of grade-school age and older, with a helpful section on ethnic celebrations.

Travnikar, Rock. *The Blessing Cup: 40 Simple Rites for Family Prayer-Celebrations*. St. Anthony Messenger Press, 1994. This resource offers a simple format for family prayer around a special cup which may seem too "churchy" for some families, but may be just right for others.

BIBLIOGRAPHY

Resources on Holidays and Saints

Chase's 1996 Calendar of Events. Contemporary Books, 1995. The most complete source for holidays of every sort, especially American ones. This book is issued annually.

The Folklore of American Holidays, edited by Margaret Read McDonald, Gale Research, 1992 and *The Folklore of World Holidays*, edited by Hinnig Cohen and Tristram Potter, Gale Research, 1987. Both are packed with plenty of information.

Foley, Leonard, OFM, ed. *Saint of the Day: Lives and Lessons for Saints and Feasts of the New Missal.* St. Anthony Messenger Press, 1990. Very clear reflections on saints of the Catholic calendar. For adults.

Hanley, Boniface, OFM. *Ten Christians.* Ave Maria Press, 1979. An excellent collection of short biographies of Pierre Toussaint, Damien De Veuster, Frederick Ozanam, Maximilian Kolbe, Mother Teresa of Calcutta, Francis of Assisi, John Bosco, Rose Hawthorne Lathrop, Joseph Cardijn and Therese of Lisieux, well-illustrated. For middle-school and older.

Koenig-Bricker, Woodene. *365 Saints: Your Daily Guide to the Wisdom and Wonder of Their Lives.* HarperSanFrancisco, 1995. A helpful attempt to apply the saints' qualities to our lives, with a reflection question and an affirmation in addition to a short reflection on each saint. For adults.

Pochocki, Ethel. *One-of-a-Kind Friends: Saints and Heroes for Kids.* St. Anthony Messenger Press, 1992. An excellent introduction to thirty Christian heroes by a skillful storyteller. For children.

ABOUT THE AUTHOR

Kathleen Finley is a noted Catholic author and speaker. She teaches in the religious studies department at Gonzaga University, primarily in the field of marriage and family. She is also the former Director of Formation, Mater Dei Institute for Ministry Formation at Gonzaga. She and her husband, author Mitch Finley, work together on various writing and speaking projects. They also work together on raising three sons.